T0145831

Opposite page: Prince Andrew.
This page: The B-26 Monument. Inset: The Carolyn.

RETURN OF THE MARAUDER MEN

Sponsored by
The B-26 Marauder
Historical Society

TURNER PUBLISHING COMPANY

TURNER PUBLISHING COMPANY
THE FRONT LINE OF MILITARY HISTORY BOOKS

Copyright © 1993 Turner Publishing Company
Publishing Consultant: David Hurst

Library of Congress Catalog Card No. 93-60442

ISBN: 978-1-68162-543-0

Additional books may be purchased directly from the publisher.

Decorations at the Essex County building May 1, 1992.

TABLE OF CONTENTS

BUCKINGHAM PALACE

I am pleased to be Patron of the 1992 USAAF Reunion which will commemorate and reinforce fifty years of remarkable friendship between two nations. During my visits to the United States I have been thrilled and encouraged by the welcome and the great kindness that has been shown to me by the American people. I have become very conscious that there is a special relationship between the British and the Americans. The presence of more than half a million American servicemen here in the 1940s helped to strengthen that relationship.

I hope that many veterans of the United States Army Forces will return to England in 1992 together with their families. A warm welcome awaits them and I hope that I may have the opportunity of meeting some of them myself.

Andrew

THE B-26 MARAUDER HISTORICAL SOCIETY

Eight B-26 Marauder bombardment groups flew and fought from British soil from late 1943 through October 1944. They then moved on to France with the advancing Allies, and a few of these became part of the army of occupation in Germany at the end of the war.

The B-26 Marauder Historical Society is composed of the men who built, maintained and flew this controversial aircraft. They were called "The Marauder Men" who it is said "succeeded against impossible odds."

The society was formed in 1988 in Dayton, Ohio, and now has over 2500 members. Their goal is to ensure that this aircraft receives its rightful place in Air Force history.

In its relatively short life span, the B-26 Marauder Historical Society has accomplished a number of significant goals, one of which is the main topic of this book, "The Return of the Marauder Men" to England and France in 1992 — the 50th anniversary of the first American warplanes arriving on British soil to help in the war against Germany. Among those first groups was the 319th Bombardment Group, and although they pre-dated by about a year the eight groups that eventually served as the bombing arm of the 9th Air Force, a small contingent from the 319th accompanied those groups back to England at the end of April 1992.

Aside from the "Return of the Marauder Men," the B-26 MHS was instrumental in 1991, after a two-year search, in the selection of a central repository for B-26 archives and memorabilia. The society chose the Bierce Library of the University of Akron, Ohio.

An agreement with the university was initialed by B-26 Marauder Historical Society President Frank G. Brewer Jr. and by Dr. Roger W. Durbin, Associate Dean, University Libraries, who represented the university.

The ink had barely dried on the agreement when Major General John Moench, who serves as the B-26 Marauder Historical Society senior historian, transferred four cartons of processed B-26 records to the archives, thus initiating a record that will continue to grow as collections already in hand are moved to the university and as Marauder persons and unit associations transfer their important accumulations of data to the archives.

The B-26 Marauder Historical Society was also instrumental in sponsoring what was the largest gathering of Marauder Men under one roof since 1945. The gathering, sponsored by the B-26 Marauder Historical Society and Martin Marietta, was held in Baltimore with more than 1,300 people attending.

The Baltimore gathering was held to honor and remember the first B-26 Marauders to roll off the assembly line in 1941.

The English 39th RAF Association (The Balkan Air Force) was present in Baltimore, led by Group Captain Frank Doran. The French were also there in force, over 40 of them, from the Les Anciens Marauders B-26 Association. They were led by Robert Camby, who spoke to the assemblage.

When the Marauder Men returned to England and France in 1992, the arrangements and hospitality shown by the English and the French were overwhelming, as readers will see in the following passages of this book.

Anyone interested in the B-26 Marauder Historical Society may write: The B-26 Marauder Historical Society, 4613 B Pinehurst Dr. So., Austin, Texas 78747, or call (512) 282-4597. The society welcomes anyone who is interested in the program.

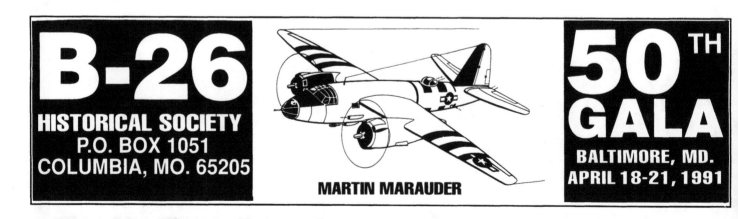

B-26 HISTORICAL SOCIETY
P.O. BOX 1051
COLUMBIA, MO. 65205

MARTIN MARAUDER

50TH GALA
BALTIMORE, MD.
APRIL 18-21, 1991

THE B-26 MARAUDER

The B-26 Marauder was much maligned when it made its debut in 1941 because the design was so advanced that none but the more experienced pilots or ground crews could handle the plane.

It was called the "Widow Maker" the "Baltimore Whore" (it had no visible means of support). It soon substantiated that claim in training in the United States where accident losses were high. So high that a Truman Committee investigating these losses recommended that the Air Force discontinue production of the plane.

The B-26 was sent into combat in early 1942 with very little testing because of the urgency of the war in the Pacific. It was sent to Alaska where the Japanese were making inroads and was sent to the Pacific where it participated in the Battle of Midway dropping torpedoes on the Japanese fleet and remained in the Pacific well into 1943.

The Marauder came into its own during the North African campaign; the 319th Bomb Group landed planes there during the initial phase of that conflict. This group that was stationed in England a short while in early 1942, was joined later by the 320th Bomb Group and the 17th Bomb Group in North Africa to operate the B-26 Marauder in a hostile environment in a very successful manner.

Accidents continued, however, in the United States at training bases in Louisiana, and Tampa, Florida, where another phrase erupted, "One-a-day-in-Tampa-Bay." It was not quite that bad, but the problems were again associated with inexperienced pilots and maintenance crews. The Air Force was rapidly developing B-26 pilot training schools at Del Rio, Texas and Dodge City, Kansas. It established ground crew training bases throughout the country. The training took valuable time and the United States didn't have too much of that in those

days. They were involved in two wars against some implacable enemies.

Martin Company stepped up the production if the B-26 Marauders during 1943 and by the end of the year a torrent of these aircraft were being sent to the European Theater of Operations where eight more fully manned groups began to combat the German forces in France in early 1944. They sustained a mighty effort for almost a year and a half, putting up more than 500 aircraft a day bombing the Fortress Europe into shambles.

They eliminated their bridges, marshalling yards, V-bomb sites (estimated 25 of them), gun emplacements and airfields. They were so effective that they drove the Germans from the coast of France enough to permit the D-Day landings on June 6, 1944 by isolating the battlefield and denying the enemy the ability to replenish his forces in Normandy.

The aircraft then established the lowest combat loss record of any American bomber during the conflict. It had proven what the initial designer, Martin's Mr. Magruder, had envisioned. It was a super safe airplane to fly and maintain when qualified persons were associated with it.

But the stigma remained. Despite its combat record, the press continued to regard the plane as unsafe, as did the Truman Committee.

Thus almost 50 years later, many of the remaining Marauder Men gathered in East Anglia to collectively remember the B-26 Marauder that served them so well and received so little recognition. They are determined that this plane receive its rightful place in history.

They were joined by their international brothers from England and France who had the same experience with the Marauder, bringing them home so shot up with flak that the skin was barely

B-26 Monument

hanging on the surfaces, yet fly them home it did and successfully. Representatives from every B-26 Marauder group that flew and fought out of East Anglia-the 322nd, 323rd, 344th, 386th, 387th, 391st, 394th and the 397th were honored by the British public throughout their visit near the villages from which they flew so long ago. This is the largest such contingent to visit England in years. There were visits to Madingley, the American Cemetery near Cambridge on Sunday, May 3, 1992.

There were also special gatherings near each of the villages on May 1, 2, and 3, 1992. This "Return of the Marauder Men", has been called the Event of the Century and will be long remembered by the unit people who are aging now. It will be lasting memory for many of them.

The timing of this celebration was particularly apropos since some of the forces involved in the recent Gulf War were English, French, and American joined for the first time since World War II to fight a common enemy.

B-26 MARAUDER HISTORICAL SOCIETY
BOARD OF DIRECTORS/SPECIAL PROJECTS

President
Frank G. Brewer, Jr.
P.O. Box 59273
Birmingham, AL 35259
323BG/456SQ
Home: 205/823-2694
Office: 205/942-1485
FAX: 205/940-9948

George W. Norris
25 Sugar Mills Circle
Fairport, NY 14450
Home: 517/369-9336
Office:
FAX: 517/369-1173

Vice President
Hugh H. Walker
4613B Pinehurst Dr. S.
Austin, TX 78747
391BG/572SQ
Home: 512/282-4597
Office:
FAX: 512/280-1761

Edward R. O'Neill
207 Dorchester Ct-POB 2074
Fairfield Glade, TN 38557
386BG/555SQ
Home: 716/223-8376
Office:
FAX:

Secretary
Nevin F. Price
P.O. Box 1786
Rockville, MD 20849-1786
397BG/599SQ
Home: 301/460-4488
Office: 301/652-2660
FAX: 301/655-1332

Esther McNaull Oyster
415 Buena Vista
Ashland, OH 44805
319BG Association
Home: 615/456-2820
Office:
FAX:

Treasurer
Richard J. Atkinson
P.O. Box 177
McCordsville, IN 46055-0177
397BG/596SQ
Home: 317/335-2636
Office:
FAX:

Video Tapes Program
Richard P. Ellinger
3245 Arcadia Place, NW
Washington, D.C. 20015
397BG/599SQ
Home: 202/966-3485
Office:
FAX:

Recording Secretary
Robert L. McKean
5 Castlehill Ct.
Timonium, MD 21093
17BG/37SQ
Home: 301/561-1084
Office:
FAX:

Senior Historian
John O. Moench
905 Sweetwater Blvd. S.
Longwood, FL 32779-3430
323BG/454SQ
Home: 407/862-5935
Office: 407/682-9113
FAX: 407/682-9113
-(call up)

Directors
Robert L. Harwell
Rt. 1, Box 57
Autaugaville, AL 36003
344BG/497SQ
Home: 205/361-1574
Office:
FAX:

Senior Archivist
Esther McNaull Oyster
415 Buena Vista
Ashland, OH 44805
319BG Association
Home: 419/289-2075
Office:
FAX: 419/289-2075

Robert L. Holliday
525 McNeilly Rd.
Pittsburgh, PA 15226-2503
391BG/573SQ
Home: 412/835-4209
Office: 412/561-7620
FAX: 412/561-7864

Immediate Past President
George W. Parker
P.O. Box 1051
Columbia, MO 65205
397BG/596SQ
Home: 314/874-3688
Office:
FAX:

Elmer Moffett
7 Foy Court
Bronson, MI 49028
Home: 419/289-2075
Office:
FAX: 419/289-2075

Frank Brewer was a member of the 323rd Bombardment Group in the ETO. He left the Army Air Corps shortly after the end of the War to join his father in the trucking business in Birmingham. He went into the electrical manufacturing business in 1961 and became President and Chairman of the Board of Dixie Electrical Manufacturing Company.

Frank got his interest in aviation from his father, Frank G. Brewer, Sr. who believed in the youth of America and their place in the aerospace world. Following his father's death in 1957, Frank Brewer, Jr., then in the CAP, approached the headquarters of the Civil Air Patrol with a request to establish a memorial in his father's name.

The Frank G. Brewer Civil Air Patrol Memorial Aerospace Awards were established on December 31, 1959 and have continued to the present.

As a Director of the B-26 Marauder Historical Society, Frank is responsible for giving B-26 models to all the museums and clubs throughout the world that he can — a big job.

Hugh H. Walker, Col. USAF (Ret) was born in Texas, but spent 30 years in California. He is married to Gladys and he has one son and one granddaughter.

He attended two years of college in Southern California. He enlisted in the Air Force in 1942 and retired from that service after 33 1/2 years, 20 years of active duty, in 1975, with the reserve rank of Brigadier General. He worked with a major Southern California newspaper as an editor and make-up supervisor while serving in a reserve capacity with the California Air National Guard. His primary job in the Air Force was in operations, completing 7,500 hours in all types of aircraft. He was active in the ETO, 54 B-26 missions, Korea, a B-45 Atomic Bomb Commander and Vietnam, with the Military Airlift Command. His last assignment was with the USAF Air Staff in the Office of the Inspector General

He became Vice President of the B-26 Marauder Historical Society in 1988 and wrote its newsletter for 3 1/2 years. He was the primary coordinator for the "Return of the Marauder Men". He did all the planning; public relations of contacting the English and the French. He also put together the text and pictures for Turner Publishing Company to print this Memory Book.

Richard J. (Dick) Atkinson, born and lived most of his life in Indianapolis, Indiana. Married to Barbara (assistant treasurer) with three daughters and nine grandchildren.

Attended Wabash College and Indiana University Extension, worked for Best Lock Corporation 41 years, 33 years as factory representative and distributor with 25 employees.

T/Sgt. radio operator/gunner in the 397th Bomb Group, 596th Squadron. Flew 67 missions with Claude Hayes crew. Served as co-chairman for 1987 and 1988 397th meeting in Dayton where the major B-26 Monument was dedicated on behalf of the B-26 Marauder Historical Society.

Became Treasurer of the B-26 MHS in 1988, three weeks after Don Kleinert, the first Treasurer, died of a heart attack.

Robert L. McKean: Board of Directors, Recording Secretary, B-26 Marauder Historical Society, 1990 to present.

Bob was a member of the 37th Squadron, 17th Bomb Group, 12th Air Force. He flew 52 missions as a Radio Operator, Aerial Gunner from Dijon, France and Corsica.

Education: Electrical Engineer with an Associate Degree in Commerical Art.

Professional: Spent 38 years with IBM as electrical engineer and manager of programs in technical and management development with assignments as a technical auditor and divisional safety manager. Prior to retirement Bob was awarded a two-year assignment as a Faculty Loan Representative at Morgan State University in Baltimore, Maryland, as an adjunct professor in Marketing and Assistant to the Dean of Business and Management.

Since retirement in 1986 he has taught at Lincoln University in Oxford, PA. and is an independent consultant in Personal and Management Development.

Community Activities: Deacon and Elder, Presbyterian Church U.S.A.; Past master-Poughkeepsie F & AM; Board of Directors - Poughkeepsie YMCA 1966-68; Occupational Education Advisory Council - Dutchess Community College, Poughkeepsie, NY 1980-83; Educational Center Task Force - Orange Community College, Newburgh, NY 1980-83; Advisory Board - School of Business and Management, Morgan State University 1985-1990; President of Mays Chapel Townhouse Homeowners Assn., Timonium, MD. 1986-88.

Married 45 years of Dorothy K. McKean. Two Children and three grandchildren (so far). Hobbies: Wood Carving, Graphic Art, Calligraphy.

RETURN TO ENGLAND

They came from every corner of the United States, just as they had fifty years earlier, when as young men — many still in their teens — they came to help stop Hitler and to prevent western Europe from being overrun by the Nazi juggernaut.

But this time there was no Hitler to stop nor war to wage. These gallant men, now grandfathers and great grandfathers, came to revisit their youth, their glory and their friends, and were literally "overwhelmed."

237 veterans of the 9th Air Force, including five representatives from the 319th Bomb Group (8th Air Force), arrived in London on April 30, 1992 for what was to be an emotional whirlwind tour of the sites in England and France from which they fought during World War II. Although the eight bomb groups that eventually made up the 9th Air Force didn't arrive until 1943, the 319th was the first B-26 Marauder group to land in England in 1942. So the occasion of the trip was also to mark the 50th anniversary of the first Marauder's arrival on English soil.

Esther Oyster, whose husband was in the 319th, and who is the B-26 Marauder Historical Society Historian, and who wrote much of the history of the 319th, was in the 319th contingency. Although the 319th Bomb Group eventually moved on to North Africa, where it participated in that invasion, some members lost their lives in England, and their names are written in the Madingley American Cemetery logs and on its "Wall of the Missing."

The day of arrival (April 30) went well. It was considered a rest day since the veterans, who arrived at staggered times throughout the morning, had traveled all night and suffered some of the effects of jet lag.

What occurred on May 1 was not only unexpected by the veterans, but set the tone for the entire trip. The Hotel Harlequin in Stansted, East Anglia had gone all out to welcome the 237 Marauder Men and their wives. The desk clerks were all decked out in military uniforms, there were sandbags on the floor and camouflage on the wall above the front desk. More than one

The Hotel Harlequin in Stansted, East Anglia went all out to welcome the Marauder Men and their wives.

Friday evening, May 1, all 237 Marauder Men and their wives were guests of the Essex County Council. (Photo by David Bartram, courtesy of Essex County Council)

Marauder Man wondered if war had been declared. It would probably be more accurate to say that friendship had been declared.

Most of the rooms for the Marauder "invasion" had been prepared, and check-in was expedited. Marauder Men and their wives filled the hotel, and a hospitality room was quickly manned

by Bob Holliday (391st) and his crew — Dick Atkinson and Nevin Price (both of the 397th) and Esther Oyster.

The Hotel Harlequin, named after the famous clown, is located next to Stansted Field. But the Marauder Men from the 344th Bomb Group, who flew out of Stansted during the war hardly recognized it. Stansted is now the third

The Essex Police Band entertained guests, American veterans and hosts at the Essex County Hall, May 1, 1992. (Photo by David Bartram, courtesy of Essex County Council)

Cas Sochocki presented Bob Mynn a special plaque, May 1, 1992. (Photo by David Bartram, courtesy of Essex County Council)

Mrs. Kathleen Nolan, Deputy Mayor, unveiled the plaque in honor of American airmen which will be hung at the entrance of County Hall, May 1, 1992. (Photo by David Bartram, county of Essex County Council)

major airport in England, and already flights to all parts of the world originate there.

That evening (Friday, May 1) was unforgettable. All 237 Marauder Men and their wives were guests of the Essex County council, and there must have been 250 of their English friends in attendance also. There was an excellent police band, and Cas Sochocki (323rd) presented Bob Mynn a special plaque. The premises were spectacular, and a wonderful repast was prepared and served. To top off the evening, a dance group comprised of young people performed the dances popular during World War II. The Marauder Men had certainly not expected such an outpouring of friendship. Some of the group were taken aside to separate rooms to be interviewed by members of the press. Press coverage was excellent wherever Marauder Men went.

And the wonderful events continued to pile up on Saturday (May 2). Early that morning, members of the group piled aboard buses and were taken to the Duxford Imperial War Museum. Then came the big surprise. They were again able to view Jack Havener's large B-26 model in front of the 9th Air Force's eight bomb group combat tail fins that were arranged on the wall. Bob Mynn had seen to their manufacture.

In front of the exhibit stood the Henry Beck (397th) B-26 pictorial. The Imperial War Museum had prevailed upon the Royal Air Force to bring the B-26 model and the pictorial to England. They made a special effort to put the exhibit together in time for viewing by the Marauder Men. It is indeed an impressive display. The museum is visited by more that 270,000 people each year. Now those visitors will have an opportunity to see some of the things the 9th Air Force and the Marauder did during the war. This is believed to be the first museum in Europe that has agreed to publicize the Marauder.

The group proceeded to lunch at the Duxford Club. There was a roll call like old times. Frank Brewer Jr. (323rd), President of the B-26 Marauder Historical Society, which was instrumental in organizing the trip, presented a special pewter B-26 Marauder to Group Captain Frank Doran, who was there with about 40 members of the 39th Association (The

Frank Brewer, Jr. presents lithograph from B-26 MHS to Mrs. Nolan, May 1, 1992. (Photo by David Bartram, courtesy of Essex County Council)

Frank Brewer, Jr. receives citation from Mrs. Nolan, Deputy Mayor of Chelmsford. (Photo by David Bartram courtesy of Essex County Council)

English children danced to Glenn Miller WW II tunes in finale entertainment at the Essex County Hall, May 1, 1992. (Photo by David Bartram, courtesy of Essex County Council)

L to R: Jack Mullin and George Parker at Duxford May 2, 1992.

Jack Havener's B-26 model in Duxford Imperial War Museum.

One of the many exhibits at the Duxford Imperial War Museum.

Balkan Air Force). Speakers included Mr. Lee of the Duxford Air Museum and Lt. Col Storie-Pugh of the British Royal Legion, the preparers of our Madingley Sunday services.

Trevor Allen — the English B-26 expert, who had joined Major General John Moench and other authors in a B-26 conference that had ended on the day the Marauder Men were flying to London — presented an excellent summary of that conference. He introduced Dr. Akers of Akron University who was a guest of the B-26 Marauder Historical Society.

Col. Brotzman, Third Air Force Deputy Commander for Plans, and representing the U.S. Embassy, ended the luncheon with an exceptional speech about the world picture from the point of view of the Air Force, and how the fall of communism will cause major changes in the U.S. presence in England. The Third Air Force is headquartered in Mildenhall. Ironically, the Mildenhall publication is called the Marauder.

It was only 12:30 p.m. and the village residents were waiting to greet the Marauder Men. The remainder of the afternoon was spent by members of the individual groups touring the areas from which they had flown during the war.

The 69 members of the 391st were greeted at Matching by a caravan of GI Jeeps, and a World War II vintage ambulance and carryalls. They escorted the buses to a special area on the old Matching Green airport (now a farm) where Bob Mynn had prepared a monument to be dedicated that day. (More about that in the individual story of the group's trip).

Each of the other groups: 322nd, 323rd, 344th, 386th, 387th, 394th, and 397th all had equally interesting stories to tell about their receptions. Those will be recounted in individual sections also.

On Sunday, the entire group traveled

Part of the 9th Air Force's exhibit at the Duxford Imperial War Museum.

Hugh Walker listens as a pastor gives the invocation, May 2, 1992.

Cake with the inscription. "Welcome Back 391st Bomb Group. Remember their brothers who laid down their lives for FREEDOM." The cake was for an evening reception given for the 391st Bomb Group at Matching Green.

This sign greeted the Marauder Men and their wives.

A B-26 Marauder (397th) pictorial exhibit at the Duxford War Museum.

by bus to the American Cemetery at Madingley where a special service had been prepared for the Marauder Men by the Royal British Legion. The weather was sunny and clear as members of the eight groups entered the cemetery.

The B-26 Marauder Historical Society had worked closely with the Royal British Legion, particularly Lt. Col. Storie-Pugh, who with his competent staff, prepared the whole visit to Madingley. They provided the speakers and information for each of them, and arranged a fly-by with the 3rd Air Force. They even rehearsed the entire program on April 29. The ceremony was perfect in the beautiful setting of the Madingley Cemetery where more than 90 men of the eight groups are buried. There are also over 65 names on the "Wall of the Missing." In addition, two members of the 319th are buried there, and they have 12 additional names on the "Wall of the Missing."

The Marauder Men returned from the Madingley ceremony in a somber mood, but their spirits were revived that evening in Colchester. The B-26 Marauder Historical Society hosted a gathering of all 237 Marauder Men, their wives and English citizens from all the villages. Bob Mynn was given a special award for his services. Frank Brewer, President of the B-26 Marauder Historical Society, introduced author Roger Freeman, who delivered an excellent speech. Ralph Bennett, the European tour agent and Kent Snyder, the U.S. tour agent, who together arranged the trip, were introduced and given a rousing hand. After a delightful buffet dinner, the tables were cleared and a Glenn Miller style band played all the music of the 1940s. The Marauder Men, their wives and guests danced the remainder of the evening.

The Marauder Men were advised to check out of their rooms in advance so there wouldn't be a jam at the Harlequin Hotel desk the next morning. Most of the group, 190, would continue on to France on Monday morning. The remainder planned either to stay in England or return to the U.S. on May 5th. Those who remained had prepared individual tours through Kent Snyder and would return at various intervals on their own.

The American Cemetery at Madingley.

The Marauder Men and their wives gather for the ceremonies at the American Cemetery on May 3, 1992.

The RAF band plays during the ceremony at Madingley on May 3, 1992.

Col. Riddick, Vice-Commander, 3rd Air Force from Mildenhall representing USAF and the American Embassy, May 3, 1992 at Madingley.

Wreaths placed in memory of departed airmen, May 3, 1992.

A fly-by with the 3rd Air Force at Madingley, May 3, 1992.

Ceremonies at the Colchester Leisure Centre, May 3, 1992. Hugh Walker presented a special award to Bob Mynn for his services.

Hugh Walker and C.V. Sochocki at the Colchester Leisure Centre, May 3, 1992.

The Marauder Men returned from the Madingley ceremony in a somber mood, but their spirits were revived that evening in Colchester. The B-26 Marauder Historical Society hosted a gathering of all 237 Marauder Men, their wives and English citizens from all the villages.

Roger Freeman (L) noted writer about B-26 aircraft, George Parker (C) 397th member and former president of the B-26 MHS and Hugh Walker (seated) Coordinator for Return of the Marauder Men visit during the gathering at Colchester, May 3, 1992.

ON TO FRANCE

After going through customs again, the 190 Marauder Men loaded aboard a chartered Boeing 737. After a small mechanical difficulty, the Marauder Men were off to Cherbourg via the Normandy invasion beaches. Madame B-Muller had prepared extensive celebrations for their arrival.

Members of the 737 crew were given B-26 Marauder hats at Richard Atkinson's suggestion, and the captain gave the Marauder Men an extensive tour of the invasion beaches in such a way as to allow those seated on both sides of the plane to view Utah and Omaha beaches. It was a very different atmosphere from June 6, 1944. When the men landed at Cherbourg, they were amazed at the extent of the preparations for their arrival.

The French Minister of Transportation was on hand, along with French troops in military formation. The Marauder Men were astonished. There was rededication of the 9th Air Force Monument at Maupertus, the airport where the 387th Group had flown from in October 1944.

When that ceremony was over, waiting buses took the Marauder Men to Lassay, where they were greeted by the city's mayor, and the men joined in a wine-tasting at the town hall. From there, the men were transported to Lindbergh Airfield (now the name of the military airport from which the 323rd flew in 1944) where the 323rd Bomb Group's

new monument was being dedicated. There followed an extensive dedication ceremony involving the French military and a band playing the national anthems of the United States and France. It was apparent that the Marauder Men were guests of the French government. All 190 members of the group attended the ceremonies, but after a lunch in one of the

French soldiers stand at attention during ceremonies at Maupertus, Cherbourg airport, during May 4, 1992 dedication there honoring the 387th Bomb Group which flew from that airfield in 1944.

May 6, 1992. 190 B-26 Marauder Historical Society and French friends in front of the ceremonial door Hotel de Ville in Paris. M. Debras (center, kneeling with dark cap) organizer of French participation in Paris.

General Lechais, our host at the Hotel de Ville, in Paris, welcomes the Marauder Men and receives the picture that the B-26 Marauder Historical Society presents to him. Background, L to R: Robert Camby, Frank Brewer - President of the B-26 MHS, General Van Hinh - President of the Les Ancien Marauders and Ralph Bennett, our European Tourist representative (holding the picture).

General Van Hinh clasps hands with Hugh Walker as M. Debras (center) and Robert Camby look on in the Hotel de Ville, Paris May 6, 1992.

General Lechais and Robert Camby chat in the Hotel de Ville. The General was the host there during the "Return of the Marauder Men" on May 6, 1992.

hangars at the airport, the Marauder Men split up to go their own separate ways.

The 397th went on the Gorges where another formal dedication had been prepared with a high mass as part of the ceremony. The members of the 394th then went back to Bayeux where there was the rededication of their monument.

The 36 members of the 391st traveled by bus to Valognes where the mayor assisted in the dedication of a new plaque built into a restored church that had been devastated during the war. Now the restoration will include a plaque in memory of Gus Kjosness, a bombardier from the 391st who lost his life over Valognes on June 8, 1944.

Each of the groups was sent on a separate tour so they could all attend a ceremony at the Normandy Cemetery where a number of the groups' members were buried. A wreath was dedicated there in memory of the 391st Bomb Group for all the 9th Air Force and 319th Bomb Group people who would visit the memorial over the next few days.

The memorials and support activities were prepared by the French-American 9th Air Force Airfields Association. The Les Anciens Marauders were there to assist them and the Marauder Men. Robert Canby, M.J. Debras and Madame B-Muller all had a hand in the celebrations. Without the help of Ralph Bennett, the European travel agent, things could not have been as well coordinated. Bennett traveled to France and consulted with Madame B-Muller and actually clocked all the distances the eight groups had to travel to be in time for each ceremony.

All 190 Marauder Men spent the night in Normandy. Each group then went its own way, because only four groups flew out of Normandy. The remaining four proceeded to Paris and on May 6 visited their old airfields.

Madame B-Muller had called ahead to prepare the local villages for the arrival of the Marauder Men. The men of the 391st were met on the morning of May 6 by a number of excited Frenchmen. Four of them joined the group at Roy-Ami. They toured the area to see the changes that have occurred since the group flew from there in October 1944. It was also the area from which they flew on December 23, 1944, when they lost 16 airplanes during the Battle of the Bulge. This was a very special place for many of those on the bus.

L to R: Hugh Walker and M. Debras at the Hotel de Ville.

"Wonderful Gesture of Comradeship." Hands on the shoulders of Gen. Van Hinh are (L) Frank Brewer, Jr. and (R) Maj. Gen. J. Moench as they rekindle the eternal flame at the Arc de Triomphe.

The B-26 Marauder Historical Society wreath at the Arc de Triomphe, Paris, May 6, 1992.

All 190 of the group met up in front of the Hotel de Ville (the town hall of Paris) at 4 p.m. on May 6 for a mass picture of the entire group. All of them then entered the Hotel de Ville through the front door. Robert Canby told the group that the front entrance is only used four times a year, and that this was an unprecedented honor.

The group was given a tour of the Hotel, a magnificent edifice that was Marie Antoinette's palace during the French Revolution. Eyes opened wide at the grandeur, the enormous rooms and the magnificent portraits. All the great chandeliers were lighted for the Marauder Men. It was difficult to absorb all of it.

The group was then bussed to the Arc de Triomphe. The American warriors then trod slowly over the road to the arch as the police actually stopped traffic for 15 minutes while the Marauder Men entered the arch and participated in rekindling the eternal flame.

Thus ended the overwhelming, exhilarating and nostalgic 1992 "Return of the Marauder Men." More detailed accounts of the trips of each individual group follows.

A little discussed date was that the Marauder Men were leaving on May 7, 1992, 48 years to the day after Germany surrendered. The official signing of the surrender was on May 8, but the Germans actually surrendered the day before.

There were some other strange and significant happenings on the trip. Several men discovered graves of friends who had lost their lives in Europe. They had just discovered their records after all these years.

Members of the 397th, visiting one of the cemeteries, discovered two men from the 386th who had been listed as missing all these years had been found and identified just recently, and the families were being notified.

Almost as strange was the discovery that there was a living member of the 391st on the trip who had received the Distinguished Service Cross for shooting down five German airplanes in the Battle of the Bulge. Wes Loegering had not discussed this decoration for fear the airlines would not hire a man who had been wounded. He finished a career with the airlines and now does not mind it being discussed and honored.

Return of the Marauder Men Attendee List

AU Akers, Stanley   Akers, Sarah
344 Andrews, William   Andrews, Edna
387 Arp, Howard
397 Atkinson, Richard   Atkinson, Barbara
RAF Ayling, Mr. A.   Ayling, Mrs. A.
397 Berry, Don   Berry, Virginia
394 Blakely, Russell   Blakely, Mary Lou
323 Blumenthal, Manfred   Blumenthal, Sylvia
391 Blute, John   Blute, Virginia
391 Bonde, P.K.   Bonde, Gloria
397 Boyar, Bradford   Boyar, Estella
397 Bresler, George
323 Brewer, Frank   Brewer, Anne
323 Brier, William   Brier, Geraldinge
391 Brooks, William   Brooks, Marion
397 Buettner, Warren   Buettner, Rose
RAF Burdett, Mr. O.
322 Burke, Harold   Burke, Ruth
RAF Callum, Mr. J.
323 Cassano, Nelzo   Cassono, Verona
323 Caswell, William   Caswell, Priscilla
394 Centanino, Frank   Centanino, Fay
397 Chacos, Nicholas   Chacos, Theresa
397 Christian, George
397 Christiansen, Rudy   Christiansen, Cathy
391 Clark, Allen
319 Coffey, Frank   Coffey, Florence
323 Conkling, John   Conkling, Katherine
319 Connaughton, Joseph   Connaughton, Laura
394 Connelly, John   Connelly, Carolyn
397 Cook, Erwin
344 Corcoran, Tressa
391 Cox, Robert
RAF Davis, B.E..
387 DeLong, James
344 Dobson, William   Dobson, Darla
RAF Doran, Frank   Doran, Sylvia
391 Dragonette, John   Dragonette, Catherine
RAF Draper, Rev. A.J.
RAF Dunlop, Mr. J.
397 Eggleston, Glenn
386 Elam, Rodes   Elam, Geraldine
344 Eldridge, George   Eldridge, Elena
397 Ellinger, Richard
397 Ellinghaus, Fred   Ellinghaus, Kathleen
323 Fehlman, Leo
391 Fetters, Wendell   Fetters, Jean
387 Firebaugh, Max
344 Freeman, Russ   Freeman, Helen
391 Fry, Donald   Fry, Millicent
391 Garwick, Robert   Garwick, Catherine
387 George, Joseph   George, Analee
322 Goetz, Bill   Goetz, Katherine
391 Goodlander, Oliver
397 Graham, Wallace   Graham, Donzella
391 Graves, William   Graves, Ann

391 Harrington, William   Harrington, Nancy
323 Harris, Billie   Harris, Paula
344 Harwell, Bob   Harwell, Helen
RAF Hatcher, Mr. P.   Hatcher, Mrs. P.
RAF Hawkins, Mr. O.
397 Hayes, Claude   Hayes, Margaret
344 Healy, Mary
386 Hellen, Robert
387 Henderson, Jim   Henderson, Audrey
344 Hillis Edward   Hillis, Jo
391 Hinds, Robert   Hinds, Helen
397 Hockey, Betty
391 Holliday, Robert
397 Howard, George
394 Howerton, Doris
394 Jackson, Joseph   Jackson, Adria
391 Jacobson, Willard   Jacobson, Carol
344 Johnson, Kay
323 Jones, James
RAF Kennedy, Mr. P.
RAF Kinch, Mr. A.   Kinch, Mrs. A.
397 King, Frederick   King, Helen
RAF King, Mr. G.
387 Kovalchik, Edward
344 Landsdowne, Owen   Landsdowne, Elvora
322 Lane, George   Lane, Joan
RAF Lane, Mr. R.   Lane, Mrs. R.
391 Lanford, Edwin   Lanford, Anne
RAF Lashbrook, D.W.   Lashbrook, M.L.
323 Lennox, Christopher   Lennox, Rosemary
322 Levy, Harold   Levy, Romona
344 Lewman, Rodney   Lewman, Vera
322 Locke, Kenneth   Locke, Myrtle
391 Loergering, Weston
397 Looker, Edward   Looker, Ellen
391 Lowenthal, Sam   Lowenthal, Lona
391 Lubin, Sam   Lubin, Marilyn
323 Madara, Richard   Madara, Sonnet
323 Mancuso, Frank   Mancuso, Clara
391 Marines, Arch   Marines, Virginia
RAF McCausland, Mr. O.   McCausland, Mrs. O.
391 McCreary, Donald   McCreary, Adele
391 Mikkola, George
323 Miller, William
RAF Millin, Mr. J.   Millin, Mrs. J.
323 Mingus, Frederick
323 Moench, John   Moench, Mary
RAF Moore, Mr. E.   Moore, Mrs. E.
322 Morrison, John   Morrison, Bobbie
391 Moscovic, Frank   Muscovic, Margerite
323 Mustacciuolo, John   Mustacciuolo, Doris
RAF Newcombe, Edward
391 Nichols, LeRoy   Nichols, Frances
322 Norstrom, Svenn   Norstrom, Helen
319 Oyster, Esther

397 Parker, George   Parker, Lois
387 Paukert Robert
RAF Payton, Mr. T.   Payton, Guest
RAF Perrett, Mr. G.
391 Perry, Naurbon   Perry, James
391 Perry, Riaford   Perry, Lillian
323 Petrasek, Fred   Petrasek, Virginia
391 Petrich, Michael   Petrich, Millicent
391 Phillips, Bill   Phillips, Frances
323 Pilmer, Charles
397 Price, Nevin
397 Pyle, Robert   Pyle, Doris
394 Reagan, Bill   Reagan, Patricia
322 Rigg, Richard   Rigg, Evelyn
RAF Roberts, Mr. W.
397 Roccia, Ron   Roccia, Phylus
RAF Roe, Mr. M.
RAF Ross, Mr. A.
386 Rounds, Walter   Rounds, Majorie
322 Saladino, Joseph   Saladino, Mary
391 Savoni, Joseph
391 Schneider, Bob   Schneider, Helen
391 Schoerlin, George   Schoerlin, Lena
344 Schwaergerl, Robert   Schwaergerl, Wilma
323 Sellier, Bill   Sellier, Elizabeth
RAF Shaw, Mr. O.
387 Skotarczyk, Walter
397 Slovachek, Charles
387 Smith, Robert
323 Sochocki, C.V.
323 Spradling, George   Spradling, Marge
344 Stalter, James   Stalter, Barbara
391 Stanford, Lester   Stanford, Mary
RAF Sutton, Mr. K.   Sutton, Mrs. K.
RAF Swan, Mr. F.   Swan, Mrs. F.
344 Tancordo, Ralph   Tancordo, Mary
387 Taylor, Harry
RAF Tennant, Mr. R.   Tennant, Mrs. R.
344 Thomas, James III   Thomas, Betty
319 Thomas, Perry   Thomas, Geraldine
397 VonGal, Don
391 Walker, Hugh
323 Weaver, George   Weaver, Barbara
RAF Webster, Mr. M.   Webster, Mrs. M.
344 Weidner, Leo   Weidner, Agnes
397 Wentz, Fred   Wentz, Elizabeth
RAF West, Mr. K.   West, Mrs. K.
391 Wetherbee, Dana   Weatherbee, Althea
RAF Wheeler, Mr. B.
322 Williams, Bill   Williams, Carol
323 Williams, Lewis
391 Wilson, Clair   Wilson, Ruth
323 Wood, Evelyn
391 Wright, William   Wright, Barbara
397 Yingling, Joe   Yingling, Dorothy

17

319TH BOMBARDMENT GROUP

Squadrons: 437th, 438th, 439th, 440th

Brief WW II History

Although the 319th Bombardment Group was not part of the 9th Air Force during World War II, it was the first B-26 unit to touch down in England, hence the group was accorded a special place during "The Return of the Marauder Men" in 1992, 50 years after that historic event.

Esther Oyster was in the 319th contingent. She is the B-26 Marauder Historical Society historian. Her husband was a member of the 319th, and she also wrote much of the 319th history. Although the 319th eventually participated in the invasion of North Africa, some members of this group lost their lives transiting England. Their names are written in the Madingley American Cemetery and on its "Wall of the Missing."

The group was constituted as the 319th Bombardment Group (medium) on June 19, 1942 and was activated on June 26. The group trained with B-26s, and moved via England to the Mediterranean Theatre during August through November of that year, with part of the group landing at Arzeu beach during the invasion of North Africa on November 8.

The group operated with the 12th Air Force until January 1945, except for a brief assignment to the 15th Air Force between November 1943 and through January 1945.

The group began combat in November 1942, attacking airdromes, harbors, rail facilities, and other targets in Tunisia until February 1943. The 319th also struck shipping to prevent supplies and reinforcements from reaching the enemy in North Africa.

After a period of reorganization and training between February and June 1943, the group resumed combat operations and participated in the reduction of Pantelleria and the campaign for Sicily. The group directed most of its attacks against targets in Italy after the fall of Sicily in August 1943. The 319th hit bridges, airdromes, marshaling yards, viaducts, gun sites, defense positions and other objectives.

The group supported forces at Salerno in September 1943, and at Anzio and Cassino between January and March 1944. The 319th carried out introductory operations in central Italy to aid the advance to Rome, and was awarded the Distinguished Unit Citation for a mission on March 3, 1944, when the group, carefully avoiding religious and cultural monuments, bombed rail facilities in the capital.

The group received a second DUC for striking marshalling yards in Florence on March 11, 1944 to disrupt rail communications between that city and Rome.

The 319th received the French Croix de Guerre with Palm for action in preparation for and in support of the Allied offensive in Italy, April-June 1944.

From July to December 1944, the group bombed bridges in the Po Valley, supported the invasion of southern France, hit targets in northern Italy, and flew some missions to Yugoslavia, converting in the meantime, in November, to the B-25 aircraft and later to the A-26 aircraft.

The group returned to the U.S. in 1945 and was redesignated as a light bombardment group. The group was then sent to Okinawa in the Pacific Theatre and assigned to the 7th Air Force, where it flew missions to Japan and China, attacking airdromes, shipping and marshalling yards, industrial centers, and other objectives.

The group returned to the U.S. in November and December 1945 and was inactivated on December 18.

Clockwise from top, 437th SQ, 439th SQ, 440th SQ, 438th SQ.

322ND BOMBARDMENT GROUP

Squadrons: 449th, 450th, 451st, 452nd

RECTE FACIENDO NEMINEM TIMEO

BRIEF WWII HISTORY

The group was constituted as the 322nd Bombardment Group (medium) on June 19, 1942, and was activated on July 17. The 322nd trained with B-26 aircraft. Part of the group moved overseas during November and December of 1942, but the planes and crews did not follow until March and April of 1943.

The group operated with the 8th Air Force until assignment to the 9th Air Force in October 1943 when it dispatched 12 planes for a minimum low-level attack on a power plant in Holland. The group sent 11 aircraft on a similar mission three days later with disastrous results. One plane returned early, while the remainder, with 60 crewmen aboard were lost to flak and interceptors.

The group then trained for medium altitude operations for several weeks and resumed combat on July 17, 1943.

The 322nd received the Distinguished Unit Citation for the period of May 14-July 24, 1943, during which its combat performance helped to prove the effectiveness of the medium bombers.

Enemy airfields in France, Belgium and Holland provided the principal targets for the 322nd from July 1943 through February 1944, but the group also attacked power stations, shipyards, construction works, marshalling yards and other targets.

Beginning in March 1944, the group bombed railroad and highway bridges, oil tanks and missile sites in preparation for the invasion of Normandy. On June 6, 1944, it hit coastal defenses and gun batteries.

Afterward, during the Normandy campaign, it pounded fuel and ammunition dumps, bridges and railroad junctions. The group also supported the Al-

lied offensive at Caen and the breakthrough at St. Lo in July.

In addition, the 322nd aided the drive of the Third Army across France in August and September. The group bombed bridges, road junctions, defended villages and ordnance depots in the assault on the Siegfried Line between October and December 1944.

The 322nd flew a number of missions against railroad bridges during the Battle of the Bulge, December 1944-January 1945, then concentrated on communications, marshalling yards and fuel dumps until its last mission on April 24, 1945.

The group moved to Germany in June 1945, where it engaged in inventorying and disassembling German Air Force equipment and facilities. The group returned to the U.S. during November and December 1945 and was inactivated on December 15.

RETURN TO GREAT SALING OF 322 BOMB GROUP 449 SQDN.

By Ken Locke

Ten members of the 322 Bomb Group, 449 Squadron and their wives arrived at Great Saling and were escorted to the monument which was to be dedicated to the 322 Bomb Group. They had an Honor Guard of six young people and two members of the In Pensioners in full dress uniforms. The Vicar of the St. Mary Church, the Rev. John Sutton, did the moving service. It began to rain and was cold, but everyone stayed for the service. After the ceremony, the Vicar gave his church's old flag to the 322 Group. We are really proud of this flag.

After the ceremony, we were taken to Andrews Airfield where we were interviewed and shown around. We couldn't determine where our barracks or anything else had been, they showed us where the runway had been.

The local people had prepared a bulletin board for all of us to sign and had a poster, "Lock up all the grannies, the Yanks are coming." We all had a laugh over that. After coffee and soft drinks there we had a fly-over of a "Spitfire." Several of our group went up for a ride. As we were leaving the airfield, the pilot buzzed our bus a number of times and put on a real show for us.

They then took us to Stebbing for further entertainment. Stebbing is one of the really old villages in England and everything remains as it was in the past. The wives were invited for sherry and a warm fire in one of the 550-year-old homes. They thoroughly enjoyed this visit. The men were taken to see the old St. Mary Church, built in the early 14th century, and then to see the old 450-year-old "Red Lion Pub" which had been turned into a home. The owner is tall and couldn't live in the home without having work done to give the ceilings more height. It couldn't be changed outside, so they dug down six inches into the ground and put in new flooring. All the homes looked as they did hundreds of years ago. This was a treat for us.

Then we went to the local pub for a welcoming party. We had a tasty dinner and cake decorated in red, white and blue. When the meal was over, they welcomed us with speeches and gifts to each couple. They gave us a hand painted card with a special Queen Elizabeth Stamp, two books Andrews Field and Warbirds, and another special "canceled" Queen Elizabeth stamp.

The two In-Pensioners, wearing their uniforms, (who live at the Royal Hospital in Chelsea as retired British military) gave the 449th Squadron a plaque.

Then there were a couple of singers who led us in a sing-along which we enjoyed very much. They also sang for us. One of the singers was named Marilyn. She had entertained the women in her home.

The bartender said there had never

Above and below, welcoming signs for the 322nd in the airport tower at Great Saling, England. (Photos by Ken Locke)

Dedication of Memorial to the 322nd BG by the people of Great Saling and Stebbings, England. Pictured, Harold Burke, Ken Locke, John Morrison, Swede Monstrom, Harold Levy, Bill Williams, Richard Rigg, Joe Saladino, George Lane, all of 322nd BG, 449th SQ. (Photo by Ken Locke)

Young British cadets at the dedication of Memorial at Great Saling, England to the men of the 322nd BG, May 1992. (Photo by Ken Locke)

been so many people in the pub at one time. We really didn't want to leave. Everyone was so friendly and wanted to talk with us.

One English couple, Mick and Joan Sargent drove about 100 miles from Norfolk, England to meet and visit with the group. They were with us at the dedication of the monument on through the evening at the pub. They did not want to leave, but had to drive back home to Norfolk.

Another couple with their two young sons were there when we arrived at the monument, through the party at the pub and again the next day at the laying of the wreath at Madingley Cemetery. The young man was the owner and pilot of the Spitfire. Their two sons were very knowledgeable about the history of Stebbing. We gave each of the boys a B-26 Historical Society cap and later sent the father another. They were very proud.

Mr. and Mrs. John Regan and the others in charge, and the local people were extremely nice to us all day. The Regans and Mrs. Cox had been at the reception the night before at Chelmsford, Essex County. We certainly enjoyed our visit there at Great Saling, Stebbing and all of the places we saw in England.

We left Paris and went to Beauvais Tille Airfield. One of the Frenchmen, Jacques Maillard, who had lived close to the airfield during the war got on the bus when we got to town. He couldn't speak English and had his brother-in-law translate. There was another Frenchman with them. They directed us to the old airfield. We could remember better here where the barracks, hangar and other buildings had been. We saw part of the old runway. They also showed us some of the German barracks and other interesting sites at Beauvais Tille.

We were to have had lunch at the brother-in-law's restaurant in town. But in order to see the museum in Mr. Maillard's home, we didn't have time to go to the restaurant.

We went out to Mr. Maillard's home, which looked like a Swiss chalet overlooking a beautiful valley. We all secretly thought, "This couldn't be much of a museum in his home." We were pleasantly surprised. It is the "Musie De L'Aviation Aircraft Museum et Memorial 1939/45." It is a great little museum and we thoroughly enjoyed it. Mr. Maillard, not being able to speak English, pointed to an old newspaper clipping of some children sitting on a plane. He pointed to himself and then to one of the children — that was him in that picture.

Mr. Maillard's brother-in-law was not daunted by our not having time to eat at his restaurant. He just had a couple of young men bring lunch to us. They quickly set it up and we all ate heartily. Lots of cheese and wine, also. They were certainly hospitable to us.

Before we left, a doctor, living and practicing medicine in Paris, came out to visit the Group and especially two of the men, Swede Norstrom and Harold Burke. When the doctor was a child living by the airfield, he became ill with pneumonia and these two men were instrumental in getting the Flight Surgeon to go to his home and take care of him. The doctor's mother credited the two with saving his life. He came from Paris to Beauvais Tille to visit with them.

People here in the States have told us the French don't like us too well. Maybe that's true for some, but not for all. When we got on the bus to leave Mr. Maillard's home, we saw big tears running down those two Frenchmen's faces.

All in all, we wouldn't take anything for our return visit to Beauvais Tille. We plan to go back in 1994 for the 50th reunion.

The old airfield at Beauvais-Tille, France. Men from the 322nd BG, 449th SQ are Ken Locke, Harold Burke, John Morrison, Richard Rigg, Bill Goetz, Joe Saladino, Bill Williams, Harold Levy. (Photo by Ken Locke)

322 Bomb Group. London Hotel, May 1, 1992. Bill Goetz, Bill Williams, Dick Rigg, Ken Locke, George Lane.

323RD BOMBARDMENT GROUP

Squadrons: 453rd, 454th, 455th, 456th

VINCAMUS SINE TIMORIS

BRIEF WWII HISTORY

The group was constituted the 323rd Bombardment Group on July 19, 1942, was activated on August 4, and began training with B-26s. The 323rd moved to England between April and June of 1943 and was initially assigned to the 8th Air Force, and was reassigned to the 9th Air Force in October.

The group began combat operations in July 1943, attacking marshalling yards, airdromes, industrial plants, military installations, and other targets in France, Belgium and Holland. The group also carried out numerous attacks on V-weapon sites along the French coast.

The 323rd attacked airfields at Leeuwarden and Venlo in conjunction with the Allied campaign against the German Air Force and German aircraft industry during what was known as the "Big Week" of February 20-25, 1944.

The group helped prepare for the invasion of Normandy by bombing coastal defenses, marshalling yards, and airfields in France, then struck roads and coastal batteries on D-Day, June 6, 1944.

In July, the 323rd participated in the aerial barrage that assisted the breakthrough at St Lo.

In August, after moving to the continent, the group flew its first night mission, striking enemy batteries in the region of St. Malo. Also during August, the 323rd carried out other night missions to hit fuel and ammunition dumps.

The group went on to eliminate strong points at Brest in early September, then shifted operations to eastern France to support advances against the Siegfried Line.

The 323rd was awarded the Distinguished Unit Citation for actions during the Battle of the Bulge (December 24-27, 1944), when the group effectively hit transportation installations used by the enemy to bring reinforcements to the Ardennes.

The group flew introductory missions into the Ruhr and supported the drive into Germany by attacking enemy communications.

The 323rd ended combat operations in April 1945 and moved into Germany in May to participate in the disarmament program.

The group returned to the U.S. in December 1945 and was inactivated on December 12.

323RD BOMB GROUP EXPERIENCE

Unforgettable Tributes From Friends; Fast Moving Events Topping Each Other

East Anglia, May 1-3 1992 — Those who were there experienced an unforgettable event —those who missed the outpouring of recollection and appreciation from the English and French citizenry will be forever sorry.

But, before we get to England and France, everyone from the 323rd Group should know that we tried—we tried hard to find the Orphan Dawn. Supported by Ken West and Derek Dempster in the U.K. and with BBC and other media working on our behalf, we eventually learned the full name of Dawn and traced her through to her marriage when her name changed from Wood to Murray. But, there the trail stopped and in spite of the best effort by many, the "Dawn Patrol" could find no following clue. Perhaps someday, Dawn will re-emerge with the sparkle which surrounded her in the early forties.

Back to "The Return". What does one think, do or say when entire villages turn out to greet the returning Marauder Men? And how does one react when the highest tributes are bestowed on your efforts in World War II?

The Return of the Marauder Men to England and France was a rapid fire succession of events that demonstrated the deepest of friendship and appreciation. Everyone who participated in these events was repeatedly moved to tears.

To initiate events on the first full day in England the entire assembly of Marauder men and their families and friends were hosted by local officials at the County Hall in Chelmsford. This event was a grand affair of the highest order. With TV and other coverage, we made news in England and France with eventual pick-up in the U.S. We were off to a grand start!

The next morning, Saturday, the entire group moved off to the Duxford Museum for a tour of the facilities and a lunch at the "Officer's Club." There we heard several speakers to include Trevor Allen of England who has now assumed the positions of Chairman of the Advisory Group that will oversee the B-26 Marauder archives at the University of Akron. Among other things, Trevor reported to the audience on the results of the international conference of Marauder researchers and authors that had taken place on the 30th of April. This conference was attended by Dr. Stanley Akers of the University of Akron and Dr. James Kitchen III of the Historical Research Agency at Maxwell Field.

In the afternoon of Saturday, the 323rd contingent split off from the main party to visit Earls Colne. On entering this city, immediate note was taken that an American flag flew from the village cathedral. Then as we pulled up to the cathedral grounds one was awestruck for there on the sidewalk stood a great collection of the villagers. Initial greetings over the villagers individually escorted us through the city, to our favorite pubs and back in time for Cas Sochocki to officiate at a tree planting in our honor. As would be so often the case in the days that followed, there was just not enough time.

From the village cathedral we proceeded under escort of a WWII convoy

The program printed for welcoming the 323th Bomb Group to Coggeshall.

of British persons in U.S. uniform manning mint condition WWII vehicles to the Rebel Air Museum—there to be greeted by a school marching group. Inside the museum there were items to unveil and dedicate and more. But again the clock turned and we were off to a tea hosted by Mr. Hobbs, present owner of the golf course, that now occupies the old Earls Colne airfield. En route to the clubhouse, we were thrilled by the low level flying and acrobatics of a YAK.

In Mr. Hobbs' clubhouse, we found an unsurpassed spread of food and more. Adorning the walls were framed photos of 323rd Group men and events. Finally, we had to leave but it was only, once again, to be overcome by the hospitality we had encountered. First, however, we traveled to the 1-10th airfield constructed on the property where there is located a formidable obelisk on which the 323rd plaque was dedicated in a most moving ceremony. Then, on Coggeshall, we found the town meeting hall crammed with villagers who provided for us an almost 100 foot table of open-dish delicacies prepared by the individual families. With food, wine and friendly conversation flowing everywhere, we eventually headed for our hotel and some earned rest.

The next morning, Sunday, we were off to the Madingley Cemetery where we participated in a most heart-tearing ceremony in honor of those who were not with us. Punctuated by a fly-over of aircraft, it was difficult to find words to express one's feelings. That evening we were given a farewell dinner at Colchester, a Glenn Miller Band provided the music, and Roger Freeman, noted British Marauder author, kept us in stitches with his recollections of what it was like in the forties.

By the time we left England everyone thought we had reached the ultimate in whirlwind events and hospitality but we would be wrong.

Cherbourg, Lessay, Paris. May 4-8 1992—Flying to France in a charter aircraft, the pilot managed to give us a low-level view of the Utah and Omaha invasion beaches. Than, on landing at Maupertus airport in Cherbourg, we attended a rededication of the monument in memory of the 387th Bomb Group which flew from there in October 1944. We found troops, school chil-

The Town Hall was decorated for the Return.

Casimier V. Sochocki and Mr. John Perks at tree planting in honor of the 323rd BG.

Ready to leave the Reference Hotel going to the lighting ceremony. Sochocki, Oyster, Jones, Williams, Miller, the English tour manager and Manny Blumenthal.

Placing flowers on the Memorial at Lessay.

The obelisk above will be the focal point of a six acre memorial.

Rod Leuruan was honored with a real Bobby helmet, jacket and whistle.

dren, citizens—the whole community—waiting for us. Immediately on arrival, each Marauder Man was given a bag which in the French tradition of hospitality, included packages of butter, one of cheese, and a bottle of cider or wine. A massive lunch had been set for us in one of their hangars—more than anyone could eat—and then moved to dedicate a monument with the 323rd plaque—this in a most colorful and tearful ceremony that was capped by a host of school children dressed in red, white, and blue place bouquets of flowers around the memorial. Again, a flyover punctuated the ceremony.

Following a night in Bayeux, the 323rd contingent went on to tour Omaha Beach and the St. Laurent Cemetery passing en route the somber German cemetery at Combet to Point du

Hoc where our men scaled the almost vertical cliffs against severe opposition to the memorable lunch in the village of Manche, and on to Utah Beach and St. Mere Eglise.

After a night in Paris, we were taken to the Hotel de Ville, the city town hall where the seldom-used ceremonial door was opened for us. What a tribute! But that was not all!

Following a tour and explanation of the splendor of the Hotel de Ville and a bit of champagne and snacks, we bussed to the Arc de Triomphe. There, to the amazement of all, the French police stopped traffic on the Champs Elysses and we all strolled up the avenue to the Arc. Then, at the Arc, Frank Brewer, General Van Hinh, who had led the Marauder victory flight over the Arc on V-E Day and General John Moench wielded the ceremonial sword and re-

lighted the eternal flame. That ceremony over, everyone signed the record book.

A final word. These events could not have transpired without the massive support in England of the BOTNA organization and Bob Mynn, the Essex County Council, the host of Britishers—famous persons down to the individual villagers—and in France, of Madame Bouvier-Muller, who heads the French-American 9th AF Airfields Association and of M. Debras who heads the Les Anciens Marauders, a host of Frenchmen. We had honor guards and other participants from the USAF in England and in France, ceremonial units from the RAF and French Air Force, local military organizations, many carrying their unit flags from WWII and more. Truly, the Marauder Men were honored at the highest levels one could imagine.

344TH BOMBARDMENT GROUP
Squadrons: 494th, 495th, 496th, 497th

BRIEF WWII HISTORY

The group was constituted as the 344th Bombardment Group (medium) on August 31, 1942, and activated on September 8. The group was equipped with B-26s and served for a time as a replacement training unit.

During January and February of 1944, the group moved to England and in March, began operations with the 9th Air Force. The 344th attacked airfields, missile sites, marshalling yards, submarine shelters, coastal defenses and other targets in France, Belgium and Holland.

Beginning in May, the group helped prepare for the invasion of Normandy by striking vital bridges in France. On D-Day (June 6, 1944) the 344th attacked coastal batteries at Cherbourg. During the remainder of June, it supported the drive that resulted in the seizure of Cotentin Peninsula, and also bombed defended positions to assist the British forces in the area of Caen.

The group received the Distinguished Unit Citation for a three-day action (July 24-26, 1944) against the enemy, when the group struck troop concentrations, supply dumps, a bridge, and a railroad viaduct to assist advancing ground forces at St. Lo.

The 344th knocked out bridges to hinder the enemy's withdrawal through the Falaise gap, and bombed vessels and strong points at Brest during August and September 1944.

In November, the group attacked bridges, rail lines, fortified areas, supply dumps and ordnance depots in Germany.

During December 1944 and January 1945, the 344th supported Allied forces during the Battle of the Bulge, and continued to strike such targets as supply points, communications centers, bridges, marshalling yards, roads and oil storage tanks until April.

The group made training flights and participated in air demonstrations after the war. In September 1945, the group moved into Germany as part of the United States Air Forces in Europe, and served with the army of occupation. The group began training with the A-26, but continued flying the B-26.

In December 1945, the group was redesignated as a light bombardment group. In February 1946, the group was transferred to the U.S. without personnel and equipment, and was inactivated on March 31.

344TH BOMB GROUP REVISITS EUROPE

Rod Lewman, Russ Freeman, James Thomas, George Eldridge, Robert Harwell, Bill Dobson, unidentified, Ralph Tancordo, Leo Weidner and Owen Lansdowne at plaque dedication at the Stansted Airport.

Twenty-nine former 344th Bomb Group members and wives made a 50th year return visit to England and France on April 29th through May 7th, 1992. They visited airfields from which they flew or supported the Marauder B-26 twin engine medium bombers that rained destruction on the German war machine.

After a day visit to points of interest in London, the group visited Stansted which is now London's third airport. Here Owen Lansdowne and Ralph Tancordo dedicated a B-26 bronze plaque and Robert Harwell presented a model B-26 bronze plaque and Robert Harwell presented a model B-26 to airport administrator Ron Paternoster. Lambert Austin, 344th Secretary-Treasurer was unable to attend. A long tour of the air base brought back many memories of the flights made in 1944.

An ash-tree was planted by Robert Harwell, former pilot, at the Ash Pub adjoining the base where many former 344th members visited. All the tour group participated and free beer was donated by pub owner, J.E. O'Brien. Later that day the group was feted to a dinner and 40s music in the old briefing hut. All this was a courtesy of local English friends, many who watched the planes fly in 1944-45. Several gifts were presented to the group.

Local residents and many other British friends and officials feted the group as well as all other B-26 groups to several lunches, dinners, and banquets.

A very touching occasion was a visit and wreath laying at the Madingley cemetery. Another visit of the day was to the Duxford War Museum.

The group flew charter from Stansted to Cherbourg. France where both Utah and Omaha Beaches were visited. The 344th Bomb Group was the first B-26 group over the beaches on June 6, 1944 or D-day.

A day later group members returned to airport A59 Cormeilles-en-Vexin for a real enjoyable tour of the former base. The base administrator Mr. Hever Gilles extended every courtesy possible to make this a memorable visit. A young traffic controller apprentice Franck Locog toured the base with us and interpreted for guide named

Farewell evening buffet dinner at Colchester Leisure Center May 3, 1992. Roger Freeman, speaker; Robert Harwell, 344th Bomb Group; Reg Robinson, Stansted Airport tour guide.

May 2, 1992, 334th members reviewing what was thought to be a parachute hut , Stansted Airport.

May 2, 1992, Ron Paternoster, Stansted Airport Administrator accepting model B-26 from Robert Harwell on behalf of the 344th Bomb Group.

344th Bomb Group members at farewell evening buffet, Colchester Leisure Center. Front row, L to R: Russ Freeman, Ed Hillis, Jim Stalter, Bill Andrews. 2nd row, L to R: Bill Dobson, Robert Schwaegerl, Owen Lansdowne, Rod Lewman, James Thomas, Martin. Back: Robert Harwell.

Wreaths were laid and the torch rekindled at the Arc de Triomphe, Paris.

G. Chevallereau who lived at this location through WWII.

All B-26 groups visited the Hotel de Ville for a reception by the Mayor of Paris. They later rekindled the flame to the lost warriors and laid wreaths to commemorate the occasion at the Arc de Triomphe.

A free day in Paris was enjoyed by many of the group while others returned to England. Many of the tour group took separate tours of several days in England, Belgium, Germany, Luxembourg, Holland, Switzerland and Israel.

PLAQUE PRESENTATION STANSTED AIRPORT

The 344th Bomb Group Association presented a plaque and a model B-26 to the officials of Stansted Airport in commemoration of their presence there in 1944. The program was attended by more than 100, which included the 31 representatives of the 344th Bomb Group and a large contingent from 39 Squadron - the RAF crews who flew the B-26. Several local people were in attendance as well as representatives of Stansted Airport.

Stansted Airport has remained more or less active since World War II and now has become the number three international airport for London. The terminal and all other facilities are ultra-modern, including a transit system connecting directly with London and with both Heathrow and Gatwick airports.

The program consisted of introductory remarks by the sponsor for the 344th Bomb Group, Mr. Reg Robinson, who did an outstanding job of shepherding the group through all activities. Mr. Ron Pattenoster, Operations Manager, welcomed the assemblage and also accepted the plaque and model B-26 on behalf of the airport. The 344th was well represented by Owen Lansdowne, who gave the history of the Group and introduced the other participants; by Robert Harwell, our representative on the board of directors of the B-26 Marauder Historical Society, who presented the model airplane; and by Ralph Tancordo, who presented and unveiled the plaque. The benediction was made by Chris Bishop, former Chaplain for Stansted Airport.

344th Bomb Group Historian's Message Read at Plaque Dedication Ceremony, Stansted Airport - May 1992

Greetings from the 344th Bomb Group Association and its members in the United States that were unable to participate in this very special dedication.

As historian for the group, I choose to repeat the words written in the recorded microfilmed history of the Group at the end of September 1944.

"We had occupied station 169S at Stansted for seven months during which period the 344th had engaged the enemy in a total of 146 missions and had dropped a total of 7739.58 tons of explosives on his installations from Holland to brest.

The Group had weathered well the "Battle of England" and though threatened on several occasions with this same treatment we had meted out, emerged unscathed from attack. During the early part of our stay here each night for several weeks the raiding planes of the Luftwaffe flew across our field on their way to bomb London or industrial plants at Chelmsford a few miles south of us, the detonation and flashes of their bombs making the latter place appear to be just on the fringe of our field. Our anti-aircraft batteries blazed away at them while the search-light batteries sought them out. Later in the year this type of attack was supplanted by the Flying Bomb, or "Buzz Bomb" as it was commonly called, and launched from sites a short way in from the French coast line. Hardly a night passed that these pilotless craft didn't pass over or near our field, streaking mainly for London and indiscriminate destruction of its residential section. Several of these murderous contraptions, products of the depraved mind, dove and exploded within 3 to 5 miles of our location, the blast effect often being felt on our post. Others flew over us so low their outline was clearly visible as they sped on at incredible speed, all the while emitting an orange exhaust flash from it's tube-like structure above the tail.

On 30 September, we bid adieu to England, as the fleet of transport planes

carrying all out ground personnel rose above that plucky majestic country and flew toward France.

The 344th Bomb Group made a very significant contribution to the winning of the war while stationed here at Stansted; not the least of which was the honor our Group had in leading 600 planes of the 9th Air Force in the successful bombing of Utah Beach on the Cherbourg Peninsula on D-Day. Other less publicized missions had equal significance.

Our experience and nostalgic memories of the days spent here will remain with us always and so it is appropriate that we dedicate a commemorative plaque marking the spot on which we shared that very special camaraderie that brought us here to this point in time.

Carl M. Christ, Historian
344th Bomb Group Association

Bill Dobson at the Madingley US Military Cemetery, laying a wreath in memory of lost 344th members.

Members of all B-26 groups lay wreaths at US Military Cemetery, St. Laurent, France.

Entire group having last dinner at hotel before leaving Paris. May 7, 1992.

Harold Hansen's crew including some ground crew. 344th Bomb Group, 494th Squadron. Kneeling, L to R: Lambert Austin, Top Turret; Carl Christ, Bombardier; unidentified. Standing, L to R: Sgt. Gucker, Assistant Crew Chief; Sgt. Harland Ratliff, Eng. Gunner; unidentified, Ground Crew; Little Doc, Ground Crew Armament; Harold Hansen, Pilot; DeCourcey, Co-Pilot; Henry Hankowsky, Radio-Gunner.

An ash tree is planted at Ash Pub by Robert Harwell, a member of the welcome committee and J.E. O'Brien-pub owner. Many 344th members visited this Pub while stationed at Stansted.

Helen Harwell, Elena and George Eldridge tour Paris. Invalides containing Napoleon's tomb in background. May 7, 1992.

386TH BOMBARDMENT GROUP

Squadrons: 552nd, 553rd, 554th, 555th

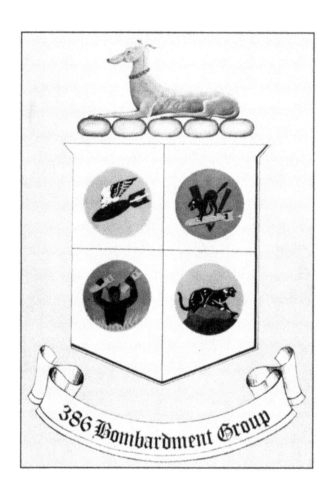

BRIEF WWII HISTORY

The group was constituted as the 386th Bombardment Group (medium) on November 25, 1942, and was activated on December 1. Equipped with the B-26, the 386th arrived in England in June 1943, and operated with the 8th Air Force until permanently assigned to the 9th in October.

The group began flying combat missions in July, concentrating on Airdomes, but also bombing marshalling yards, and gun positions.

During the winter months of 1943-44, the group carried out an extensive campaign against V-weapon sites along the French coast, and bombed airfields in Holland and Belgium during "Big Week" (February 20-25 1944).

The 386th hammered marshalling yards, gun positions and airdromes preceding the invasion of Normandy and made numerous assaults on bridges across the Seine in late May.

On D-Day, June 6, 1944, the group struck coastal batteries, and hit bridge, supply and fuel stores, gun positions and defended areas during the remainder of the Normandy campaign.

The 386th supported Allied forces at Caen, and participated in the massive blowouts against the enemy at St. Lo on July 25, 1944.

In August, the group knocked out targets to help clear the Falaise gap of German forces, and hit strong point at Brest the following month.

After moving to the continent in October 1944, the 386th attacked strong points at Metz, flew missions to Holland, and assaulted such positions as defended areas, storage depots, and communications sites in Germany.

During the Battle of the Bulge (December 1944-January 1945) the group primarily focused its attacks on bridges in order to cut off enemy supplies and reinforcements.

The group converted to A-26s shortly after the Ardennes campaign and continued to strike German communications, transportation and storage facilities until May 1945.

The group was awarded the Distinguished Unit Citation for its operations for its operations from June 1943 to June 1944.

The 386th was redesignated as a light bombardment group in June 1945, returned to the U.S. between July and August, and was inactivated on November 7.

The Top Of The Heap

Beginning in 1943 during the European Air Offensive, a mountain of destruction was levied against Germany's war machine by B-26 Marauder Groups. At the top of that decisive heap, and without peer, stands the enviable record of the 386th Bombardment Group (M). In 1944 the following Battle Honors were awarded to "The Crusaders" in recognition of their extraordinary achievements.

Battle Honors

The 386th Bombardment Group (M). For outstanding performance of duty in action against the enemy in the European Theatre of Operations from July 30, 1943 to July 30, 1944. During this period the 386th Bombardment Group (M) attained the most outstanding record of all B-26 Groups in the European Theatre of Operations in terms of number of successful sorties flown, tonnage of bombs dispatched, and enemy aircraft destroyed, while at the same time maintaining the highest bombing accuracy score. The eminently successful concentrated pattern bombing first employed by the 386th Bombardment Group (M) on 2 September 1943 established a technique in medium bombardment which was adopted with unusual success throughout subsequent operations over Western Europe, while missions of the group carried out against Amsterdam Schipol airdrome, the pilotless aircraft launching sites in the Cherboug Peninsula and the Pas de Calais area, the attacks upon marshalling yards, aircraft installations, bridges, and communications and transportation centers both prior to and during operations of the Allied Ground Forces on the Continent, were of the utmost importance to the campaign in Northwest Europe. The untiring devotion to duty and extraordinary skill and courage demonstrated by the members of the 386th Bombardment Group (M) throughout the course of these exceedingly difficult and exacting operations reflect great credit upon the entire organization and are in keeping with the highest traditions of the Service.

Rufus and Margaret Ross at the Memorial to the 386th featured at right.

A plaque on the Memorial to the 386th on Highway A120 at the edge of USAAF Station 164. It was originally built in 1948 by the Essex Anglo-American Goodwill Association. It was rededicated in 1984.

387TH BOMBARDMENT GROUP
Squadrons: 556th, 557th, 558th, 559th

A BRIEF HISTORY

The group was constituted as the 387th Bombardment Group (medium) on November 25, 1942, activated on December 1, and trained with B-26s.

The 387th moved to England in June 1943 and was temporarily assigned to the 8th Air Force, before joining the 9th in October.

The Group went into combat in August, concentrating its attacks on airdromes during its first few months of operations.

During the winter of 1943-44, the group made numerous strikes on V-weapons sites in France, and hit airfields at Leeuwarden and Venlo during "Big Week" (February 20-25, 1944), an intensive campaign against the German Air Force and German aircraft industry.

The 387th helped prepare for the invasion of Normandy by attacking coastal batteries and bridges in France during May 1944. On D-Day, June 6, the group bombed along the invasion coast and supported ground forces throughout the month by raiding railroads, bridges, road junctions, defended areas and fuel dumps.

The 387th moved to the Continent in July and participated in attacks on the enemy at St. Lo. In August and September, the group made attacks on German forces at Brest and had extended operations into Germany by the fall of 1944.

The 387th received the Distinguished Unit Citation for action during the Battle of the Bulge when the group hit strongly defended transportation and communications targets at Mayen and Prum.

The group also supported the Allied drive into the Reich by attacking bridges, communications centers, marshalling yards, storage installations and other objectives.

The 387th ended combat operations in April 1945 and returned to the U.S. in November. The group was inactivated on November 14.

THE 387TH BOMB GROUP "RETURN OF THE MARAUDER MEN" EXPERIENCE

April 29 through May 8, 1992

The 387th Bomb Group Association contingent of the "Return of the Marauder men" flew from all corners of the United States to arrive in London early in the morning April 30. After this all-night flight, we were met and whisked away to our London Hotel for a welcome recovery from "jet lag." Our hotel accommodations were awaiting us. Some of us were able to take in the London sights that afternoon and evening.

Howard Arp, Robert Paukert, Edward Kovalchik, Harry Taylor, James Henderson, Joseph George and George Anthony heard the excellent briefing given by our tour guide, Kent Snyder, the following morning. It was a pretty tight schedule. We left for East Anglia by bus Friday morning, touring London on the way to Stansted. The Hotel Harlequin was on the airport premises. The 344th Bomb Group had flown from this base near us in Chipping Ongar during the war. Now Stansted is the third international civilian airport in south England. It soon will be handling traffic from all parts of the world on a regular basis.

We were taken to the Duxford officer's club where an excellent lunch had been prepared. We left Duxford about 12:30 and journeyed with the 391st Bomb Group members to what remained of their old base at Matching Green. We arrived a little late at Chipping Ongar, our 387th World War II base. We were met by Derek Aspinwall, the director of Blake Hall, who showed us around the museum, Derek had arranged transportation for us in mint condition WW II jeeps for a tour of the village of Chipping Ongar and Willingale.

Our old air base is now owned and farmed by Mr. Alan Stock, who guided us around the premises. The perimeter roads and some hard stands are still there, plus a few Nissen huts, but the runways had been broken up to be used as fill and base for the expressways nearby.

We were then taken to St. Andrews

WW II vintage jeep found during the tour of Chipping Ongar and Willingale. Back: Harry Taylor, Howard Arp, James Henderson. Front: Joseph George, Edward Kovalchik, George Anthony and Robert Paukent.

Luncheon at Lindbergh Airport.

Cherbourg Reception.

The Blake Hall B-26 - 387th "Tiger Stripe" greeted the 387th vets at Chipping Ongar Airbase.

Cherbourg Airport. President Beatrice Bouvier-Muller bring the group to attention.

church, circa 1000, where we were met by the pupils of Class 6R of the Warley Primary School. The children interviewed us. They then presented each of us with workbooks they had made. We were overwhelmed!

That evening, we were welcomed into the beautiful restored home of Mr. and Mrs. John Calder. Their home had been a sweet shop and the Willingham Post Office in WW II. All the villagers stopped by here and wished us well. We could not have been treated better. They wined and dined us royally.

Each of us was interviewed by the local press.

A tired group arrived at the Harlequin Hotel that night.

Sunday morning, May 3, we were transported to Madingley American Cemetery for services to remember our fallen comrades there. The 387th was one of the original four B-26 marauder Groups that flew and fought out of East Anglia. There are over 24 – 387th Bomb Group members on the Madingley Wall of the Missing.

Monday, May 4, 1992. The B-26 Marauder Historical Society had chartered a large jet to transport us to France this day. After a short delay leaving Stansted, we had a great flight on a wonderfully clear day to Cherbourg (Maupertus Airfield). En route, the pilot descended to about 2,000 feet and flew along the Normandy invasion beaches for about 20 minutes, enough time for viewers on each side of the plane to see something entirely different from the D-Day memories for a lot of us.

We landed at Maupertus where the 387th Bomb Group had flown from in late 1944. We were met by an imposing group that included the French military and hundreds of civilians from the 51 villages that participated in this memorial to the 387th. The B-26 Marauder Historical Society presented a special picture to the Maupertus airport manager through George Norris, a director of the B-26 Marauder Historical Society, who was also a member of the 387th. It was presented in the name of the 387th. Also the 387th (Pat Razzano and Howard Arp) presented Madame B-Muller with a special Walter Skotarczky hand-crafted clock.

We then went on to Lessay, arriving late, but the French obtained lunch for us in a special effort. We spent the night in Normandy after a visit to St. Mere Eglise.

May 5th we toured Omaha Beach, Pointe du Hoc U.S. Ranger landing area and the beautiful St. Laurent Cemetery. The night was spent at Bayeux.

May 6th we bussed to Paris to arrive at the Hotel de Ville for the tour of this famous town hall that was once the palace of the Queen Antoinette of France. We entered through the ceremonial door that is reserved for special people. The palace is elegantly preserved and now serves as the residence of the mayor of Paris, Jacques Chirac.

That afternoon, we were brought to the Arc de Triomphe for a special rekindling of the Eternal Flame. The police stopped traffic as we marched up the Champs Elysées to stand at attention at the base that marks the site of the Unknown Soldier.

This visit was especially nostalgic for those of us who as a group flew over the Eiffel Tower on August 5, 1945 as part of a celebration of the U.S. Army Air Force Exhibition Day. Some 250 representatives of the 387th Bomb Group and their commander, Col. Philip A. Sykes were formally presented the Distinguished Unit Citation at one of the ceremonies held in the base of the Eiffel Tower.

Normandy Cemetery. Many B-26 Marauder airmen are buried here.

Members of the 387th Bomb Group visited the Normandy Cemetery.

Monument at Maupertus.

St. Mere Eglise. Note parachute hanging from the turret.

387th Bomb Group personnel at the Harlequin Hotel on Sunday, May 3, 1992. L to R: Howard Arp, Jim Henderson, Harry Taylor, Ed Kovalchik, Bob Paukert and Joe George.

Maupertus Airport manager, M. Nicollet. The new B-26 is the large picture but is behind glass so it will forever look good.

391st Bombardment Group

Squadrons: 572nd, 573rd, 574th, 575th

Brief WW II History

The 391st Medium Bombardment Group was formed on January 15, 1943 and activated six days later. Having trained with B-26 Marauders for duty with the Ninth Air Force in the European Theatre of Operations, the group moved to Matching, England during January and February of 1944.

During those dark days of the war prior to the Allied invasion of Normandy, there was no time to waste. Squadrons from the 391st flew the first of 294 missions on Feb. 15, 1944, and in the ensuing weeks bombed airfield, marshaling yards, bridges and V-weapons sites in France and the Low Countries to soften up defenses as much as possible for the invasion forces to come.

The day before the invasion and during its initial hours (June 6 and 7, 1944) the 391st pummeled enemy defensive positions along the invasion beaches, and for the next four months continued cross-channel operations, which included attacks on fuel dumps and troop concentrations in support of Allied ground troops during the breakthrough at St. Lo in July 1944. The 391st also conducted strikes on transportation and communications facilities to block the enemy's retreat to the east.

In September 1944, the group began flying its missions from the Continent, extending its operations to Germany itself, continuing its onslaught against enemy railroads, highways, troops, bridges, ammunition dumps and other targets.

One of the high points of an already distinguished career and record occurred during some of the fiercest and bloodiest fighting of the war—December 23-26, 1944, the Battle of the Bulge. The 391st contributed vital assistance to ground forces during the battle by attacking heavily defended positions without fighter escort and in the face of intense flak and overwhelming counter attacks by enemy fighters. For its performance, the group was awarded the DUC.

Between January and May 1945, and using A-26s beginning in April, the group concentrated its attacks on German transportation and communications systems. The group flew its final mission of the war on May 3, returned to the U.S. in October and was deactivated.

391ST BOMB GROUP ASSOCIATION "RETURN OF THE MARAUDER MEN" STORY

by Hugh Walker

Sixty-nine veterans and their wives of the 391st Bomb Group were astonished at the reception accorded them Friday night, May 1, 1992 at Essex County Hall where many people were present. We knew that all our group members, 237 of us, were there. It seemed as if an equal number of our English hosts were also there. All of us moved around talking avidly to each other; introducing each to the other if they didn't know that person. It was quite a change from the usual reserved person one meets in England. English friends have told us that the English are basically shy, but they were certainly overwhelming this night and this conviviality lasted throughout our visit.

Mrs. Nolan, the Essex County Council representative, exchanged gifts, plaques and pictures with Frank Brewer, Jr., president of the B-26 Marauder Historical Society. We were treated to a wonderful repast and jovial comradeship. We enjoyed the Police Band and the dancing of the young folks doing the routines of the 40s to the tunes of the 40s. We returned to the Harlequin Hotel—our headquarters at Stansted—and our B & Bs, with a feeling that was hard to explain.

Saturday early, we bussed to Duxford to see the B-26 Marauder Historical Society exhibit. This exhibit was completed just in time for our visit through much effort on the part of the Duxford staff. We viewed the eight group tail fins prepared by Bob Mynn. They were drawn in the fighting colors of the eight bomb groups which flew from East Anglia in WW II. The tail fins are a permanent gift from the B-26 MHS to the Duxford Imperial War Museum. It was an impressive display.

We observed Jack Havener's large B-26 Marauder, that had been flown over from Dulles International Airport by the RAF. This model required over 5,000 man hours to construct. In addition, we viewed Henry Beck's pictorial that had been flown over in parts and was put together by Duxford's competent staff. This display will be viewed

Harlequin Hotel, Stansted was headquarters for all eight groups, May 1 - 3, 1992.

The villagers gathered at the monument dedication at Matching Green, May 3, 1992.

A World War II Jeep leads parade at Matching.

42

The monument at Matching Green before the unveiling.

The monument at Matching Green after the unveiling.

Vets, wives and villagers at the Matching Green ceremonies.

by over 270,000 people a year for the three years the exhibit will be loaned to Duxford.

After viewing many of the Duxford exhibits, all of us were bused across the street for lunch at the Duxford Club. The proceedings there were cut short because the police were holding traffic so that the buses could transport us to the local villages where the Essex County and East Anglia people were awaiting us. We certainly did not anticipate the enthusiasm of those village people.

When our laden buses reached Matching Green, the small area from which the 391st Bomb Group took its name in World War II, our eyes opened wide looking at the WW II jeeps in mint condition. Their occupants herded us around the small green Marching Square to the area where we were to dedicate a monument to our fallen comrades. There, at the edge of our old, now closed runway, our hosts were gathered. There were many of them. We saw faces we remembered well like Wes and Gwynne Anderson, who have visited us many times in the States at our reunions. And there was Bob Mynn, our honorary historian who had built the monument. It was a beautiful tribute and the ceremony performed by the local pastor brought tears to the the eyes of us old-timers. A local band performed right there in the street that had been blocked off by the police for the ceremonies.

We then walked over to the old Matching Airfield cinema hut. It was still standing after 47 years, and had been converted to a reception hall for us. Snacks and drinks were consumed in a wonderful atmosphere of conviviality and friendship. Again, we were unprepared for such genuine outpouring of affection.

We returned to our welcomed beds for sleep and time to try to assess what had happened to us during these two days.

On Sunday, we traveled to the American Madingley Cemetery where many of our comrades are buried. All the groups were represented there. Over 90 of our airmen are buried at Madingley and many more are on the "Wall of the Missing." The 391st lost eight. Some had been removed to cemeteries in the States.

Matching Green British soldiers, May 2, 1992.

Bob Cox, Bob Mynn, Bob Holliday and the Hennesseys, May 1992. England.

The ceremonies at Madingley were most touching. It is a beautiful cemetery. The Royal Air Force and the United States Air Force supported us with a band and active service men and women, who participated in the ceremony. Many English friends were there to listen to the speakers. Tears flowed freely during Taps and the gun volleys. Eight floral wreaths from the Bomb Groups were presented in remembrance to our fallen comrades. The Royal Air Force also presented wreaths. The Royal Air Force band played some wonderful nostalgic music. At the appropriate moment, a flight of A-10s twice flew over the throng in the "missing man" formation.

These ceremonies were prepared through the diligent efforts of the Royal British Legion. Specifically, Lt. Col. Storie-Pugh, of the Queens Guard, and his staff, were responsible for the coordinating of the entire affair. It was a superb effort that will not be forgotten by our veterans.

Sunday night, the B-26 Marauder Historical Society hosted a get-together at the Colchester Leisure Centre. All our friends from the Essex County Council along with the host leaders from the villages were our guests as we tried to respond to the wonderful welcome we had received. We hoped the Glenn Miller band and the banquet would in some way demonstrate how we felt about the reception we had received during these crowded three days.

The old Cinema Hall, converted.

Bill Brooks and Hugh Walker at Matching Green monument, May 2, 1992.

FRENCH VISIT, MAY 4, THROUGH MAY 7TH, 1992

Monday morning, May 4, 190 of us were loaded into a modified 737 which was contracted to fly us to Cherbourg (Maupertus Airfield), France. Thirty-six of the 391st association members were on this plane. The pilot was asked to give us a view of the Normandy invasion coasts. We gave the crew three souvenir hats and that pilot must have flown clear down to le Havre and back at about 1,000 feet.

Our veterans on both sides of the airplane were able to view the invasion beaches. They are quiet and peaceful now. All remnants of the war had been removed with the exception of the gun emplacements that could not be seen from the air anyway.

We landed at Maupertus and were met by a large number of French people from the 51 villages that were organized by Madame B-Muller into the or-ganization which had prepared for us this day. The French Navy and Air Force were there in numbers with an honor guard and a band. The purpose of this monument rededication was in remembrance of the 387th Bomb Group, which had flown from Maupertus on steel-planked runways in 1944. At least 500 people were there, including over 40 of our friends from Les Anciens Marauders, led by its secretary, M. Debras. They planned to accompany us throughout our three day visit to France.

Our next stop was Lessay where the language barrier was a problem, but we were entertained by translated speeches by the Mayor of Lessay. There was a buffet table of snacks and wine for us.

We left the Lessay town hall for Lindbergh Airfield on the outskirts of the town, where a special monument was dedicated to the 323rd Bomb Group which had flown from that airfield in 1944. A huge crowd was present, including children who wore our red, white and blue colors. They made us welcome. Further, a delicious luncheon had been prepared in one of the hangars on the field.

At this point, the groups split up to attend functions that were planned for them in Gorges and Bayeux. Some, like the 391st, would view the Normandy Cemetery where over 17 of our com-

Mr. and Mrs. Bill Brooks near the Arc de Triomphe, Paris.

Hugh Walker, Bill Phillips, Ruth and Clair Wilson, Helen and Bob Hinds, Marion and William Brooks, Bob and Helen Schneider.

Bob Marines, Lester and Mary Stanford, Monica Locklin, (Don Locklin - hidden), Oliver Goodlander, Marguerite Muscovic, Michael and Millicent Petrich, Frank Muscovic, Naurbon Perry, James Perry, Joseph Savoni. (Not shown - Bob Holliday and Bob Cox)

Hugh Walker in Paris, France on May 6, 1992.

rades were casualties of the war. The 391st Bomb Group placed a special wreath at this monument for all the groups that would visit the cemetery in the next two days.

The 391st bus then journeyed to Valognes to dedicate a special plaque that is installed in the church entrance remembering Gustave Kjosness, a 391st/572 bombardier, who lost his life over this town on June 8, 1944. He was awarded the posthumous Distinguished Service Cross for conduct above and beyond the call to duty. The lady mayor of Valognes spoke to us there. The church services were very poignant for those who knew Gus and those who did not. A student band played the American and the French national anthems. We spent the night in Normandy and traveled on May 5, to our hotel in Paris.

Wednesday morning, the 36 members of the 391st traveled to Roy/Ami to visit the airfield they had flown out of from October, 1944 to almost the end of the war in 1945. Our bus was met by four Frenchmen, including the mayor of Roy. They escorted us back to the old areas, which are now farmland. There are few areas left that have not been converted back to their original status. After all, it had been 47 years since many of us had been there. Some remembered small places. The chateau that was the officers club was still there, closed now and overgrown with grass and weeds.

On this bus, it was discovered that Wes Loegering, 574th engineer/gunner had also received a Distinguished Service Cross. On December 23, 1944 during the Battle of the Bulge, Wes shot down five German aircraft in about 23 minutes of furious action. He is considered the only Ace gunner in the entire 9th Air Force. His story is told in detail in the 391st WW II history.

We returned to Paris in time to rest and prepare for our visit to the Hotel de Ville at 4 o'clock that afternoon. The Hotel de Ville is the old palace of Marie Antoinette, who lost her head in the French Revolution. It is now used by Mayor Jacques Chirac, who allowed the

B-26 Marauder veterans to enter the palace through the ceremonial door which is used for special celebrations only four times a year. There followed an hour-long tour of the palace. Gifts and pictures were exchanged between the French and the B-26 Marauder Historical Society President, Frank Brewer, Jr.

The palace is beautiful. Huge chandeliers were lighted for us in the very large rooms. We were accompanied throughout by members of the Les Anciens Marauder Association. This visit was conducted for the entire 190 members of our group.

Shortly afterward, we were transported to the Arch de Triomphe. The Paris police stopped traffic on the Champs Elysées to allow our veterans to slowly march to the Arch, where Maj. Gen. J. Moench, General Van Hinh and Frank Brewer, Jr. rekindled the Eternal Flame in memory of the unknown solider. It was a tremendously moving experience for all of us.

Thus ended the 391st Bomb Group's visit to the places they flew from in WW II. It was an historic visit that will not soon be forgotten. We would like to offer a special thanks to them for their participation in these ceremonies. Vive La France!

THE UNTOLD STORY OF LOEGERING'S DSC SECOND 391ST AWARD
SHOT DOWN THREE; CREDITED WITH FIVE ON DEC. 23, 1944 RAID ON AHWEILER; 391ST LOST 16
By Hugh Walker

AWARDS OF THE DISTINGUISHED SERVICE CROSS

General Orders
No. 23

Under the Provision of the Army Regulations 6—45, 22, Sept.., 1943, and circular *32 Hq. E.7.0. US. Army, 20, March, 1944, the Distinguished Service Cross is awarded to the following enlisted man:

Weston A. Loegering, 37564530, Staff Sergeant, Army Air Forces, US. Army.

For extraordinary heroism in connection with an aerial military operation against an armed enemy, 23 Dec., 1944. On this date while serving as a top turret gunner on a B-26 type aircraft, Sgt. Loegering destroyed three enemy F.W. 190s and probably destroyed two more. On their approach to the target, his aircraft was violently attacked by a large number of determined enemy fighters. They swarmed in on their formation in waves of four deep and fifteen abreast. During the ensuing battle, and after destroying two enemy fighters, Sgt. Loegering was wounded in the left shoulder. Remaining steadfastly to his guns, with one arm useless and probably bleeding severely, he destroyed a third enemy fighter, and probably destroyed two others. By his dauntless courage and

Weston Loegering, Pet and Leroy Nichols, William and Ann Graves, Margaret and George Schoerlin, Billy and Nancy Harrington, George Mikkola, In front: Jan Parsons and Pascal Leroy.

selfless devotion to duty and other members of his crew, he aided materially in the success of the attack and safe return of the aircraft.

By command of Lt. Gen. Spaatz Signed.

PARIS, MAY 6, 92—Thirty-six members of the 391st were on their bus traveling to Roy / Ami the morning of May 6, 1992. One of the passengers turned to me and said. "Did you know you have an Ace on this bus?" I did a double-take, thinking a fighter pilot had hitched a ride with us. The man was serious.

A DSC, and a Gunner ACE Award?

"Weston (Wes) Loegering was a top-turret gunner and he shot down five German aircraft on the Ahweiler raid on December 23, 1944. Not only that, but he was awarded the Distinguished Service Cross by General Spaatz."

Several members of the 391st put together the first 391st Bomb Group history when the association was formed in 1974.

All the actual yellow-aged 391st Bomb Group historical documents were sent to us by the office of history at Maxwell AFB.

History Not on Micro Film Then

They were not on micro-film nor had they been micro-filmed at that time. They came to us in a small brown box—all the records. I doubt if any of us realized the treasure we had in our hands. We only knew that the new members should be told about the contents of that box.

We immediately began the long, tedious job of microfilming those records, one page at a time. To make a long story short, we were able to put the contents into a small history book, that was published by a member who owned a print shop in Hilton Head, SC.

Old Yellow Records Did Not Show DSC

Nowhere in this book did the name of Weston Loegering appear as the recipient of the Distinguished Service Cross, much less give him credit for downing five to seven enemy aircraft on December 23, 1944.

And to this day, the 391st has not published this amazing account that occurred in 23 minutes of furious action on December 23, 1944 when the 391st lost 16 aircraft.

Well, certainly our ears pricked up at this and I talked with Weston Loegering at length about how such a thing could happen. How it was discovered after 48 years, almost by accident.

Wes Loegering's Story

Wes Loegering was an engineer-gunner in the 574th squadron of the 391st Bomb Group. He flew with Lt. Chism and trained with him at Barksdale. The crew flew as a unit over the northern route to Europe in June 1944.

They were sent to Toomebridge in Northern Ireland like many of us. Their plane was taken from them there. They joined the 391st shortly after D-day and flew a number of missions with the 574th Bomb Squadron before the 391st moved to France in October, 1944. Some 391st crew members had reached 65 missions and were sent home just as the 391st crossed the channel. Lt. Chism was slated for lead crew.

Major Loesch, the 574th operations officer, was flying as co-pilot with Chism on that fateful day when the 391st was caught without fighter cover while they were making a second run on the target after the Pathfinder aircraft had been forced out of the formation by intense and accurate flak.

Chism and Loegering in Second Box

Capt. Jennsen was leading the first box. Captain Boylan was leading the second. The taxi sheet shows Chism in the No 5 slot in the second box.

Dec. 23, 1944. That day the weather broke. Had it not broken, three aircraft from many groups were going to fly any way, at suicidal low level. There were a lot of volunteers for that mission in the 391st. Lt. Matus was one of them (shot down this day but lived to tell his story).

391st Missed Fighter Cover

Somehow, the 391st missed its fighter cover. On the second run, Wes says he looked out and saw a number of aircraft approaching. He thought initially they were ours. One came up alongside. Wes saw the German insignia on the side and immediately shot him down. He quickly shot down two more. He is given credit for two more probables. Wes was wounded after shooting down the first two planes.

He continued shooting with one arm and destroyed another German and two more. Wes says he thought he got two more than he was credited for.

Chism Made It Back; 125 Holes in AC

Wes was taken to the hospital. While he was there, the German troops caused a quick hospital evacuation and Wes was sent back to the squadron. He volunteered to fly again because of the shortage of crews and did. He still had a bullet in his shoulder as he flew on Dec. 25, '44.

Living DSC Holder Big News in US

The Award of the Distinguished Service Cross to a living crew member who had been in the battle to repulse Hitler's troops at the Battle of the Bulge made big news back in the States. Wes was sent back and participated in a big heroes' celebration in Atlanta, Georgia. Now Wes was transferred from the 391st on PCS orders to the 409th, an A-20 outfit, as it was being inactivated. He had enough points to leave but his records were part of the 409th.

Wes Loegering a Quiet Man

Wes was a very quiet, reticent man. He is reticent even now. He says the real heroes are the ones buried in the cemeteries all over the Continent.

So why haven't we known of this award? Why wasn't it listed in the 391st history records?

One of the main reasons was the assignment to the 409th as he was discharged.

The other reason was that he didn't want the airlines to know about his injury. So, he kept quiet about it all these years and retired from United Airlines as an engineer.

Wes Loegering has sent us all his award records and his discharge. We hope we can rectify the omission of his wonderful service with this account and others later.

394th Bombardment Group

Squadrons: 584th, 585th, 586th, 587th

Brief WW II History

Constituted as the 394th Bombardment Group (medium) on February 15, 1943, the group was activated on March 5, and trained with B-26s before moving to England a year later (February-March 1944) and being assigned to the 9th Air Force.

The 394th entered combat in March 1944 and helped prepare for the invasion of Normandy by hitting V-weapon sites, marshalling yards, bridges, airdromes and gun emplacements.

On D-Day, June 6, 1944, the group bombed gun positions at Cherbourg, and afterward struck communications, fuel supplies and strong points in support of the Normandy campaign.

The 394th aided the breakthrough at St. Lo. by bombing targets in the area on July 25, 1944.

The group received the Distinguished Unit Citation for operations from August 7-9 when it made five attacks against strongly fortified targets in northern France, knocking out an ammunition dump and four railroad bridges.

Captain Darrell R. Lindsey was awarded the Congressional Medal of Honor for leading a formation of B-26s over one of these bridges on August 9. During the flight, Lindsey's plane was hit and the right engine burst into flames. Knowing that the gasoline tanks could explode at any moment, he continued to lead the formation until the bomb run had been made, then ordered his crew to bail out. The bombardier, the last man to leave the plane, offered to lower the wheels so that Lindsey might escape through the nose of the aircraft, but realizing this could throw the plane into a spin and hinder the bombardier's chances to escape, Lindsey refused the offer and remained with his B-26 until it crashed.

After moving to the Continent in late August 1944, the 394th hit strong points at Brest and then began to operate against targets in Germany.

The group took part in the Battle of the Bulge (December 1944-January 1945) by hitting communications to deprive the enemy of supplies and reinforcements. It bombed transportation, storage facilities, and other objectives until the war ended, and also dropped propaganda leaflets.

The 394th remained in the theatre to serve with the United State Air Forces in Europe as part of the army of occupation. The group was re-designated as a light bombardment group in December 1945 and began training with A-26s.

The 394th was transferred without personnel or equipment to the United States on February 15, 1946 and was inactivated on March 31.

Return Of The Marauder Men - The 394th Bombardment Group To Boreham

A group of American Army Air Force veterans, former members of the 394th Bombardment Group (M), 9th USAAF, and accompanied by their wives, returned to Boreham's old wartime airfield on a nostalgic visit during Saturday 2 May 1992.

This was part of the "Return to England" reunion, commemorating the 50th anniversary of the first American servicemen to arrive in England during World War II to build airfield in East Anglia.

The party arrived at Boreham on Saturday afternoon, following a visit to the Imperial War Museum Duxford, where they viewed wartime American aircraft and other interesting exhibits. Lunch was taken in the officers mess.

First call in the village was to the Queen's Head pub, where, accompanied by members of the Parish Council, and local village people, Roger & Margaret Smith served the Americans to their particular choice in drinks.

This was followed by a tree planting ceremony on the green alongside "Coopers" and was carried out by Duane "Wild Bill" Reagan, a former navigator in 587 squadron, now living in Washington.

The Rev. David King, vicar of Boreham, then escorted the visitors around the church and where they saw the American flag, hanging as a memorial to the 64 American servicemen who died during their service at Boreham.

English style tea parties followed, when the visitors were entertained in the homes of various village families.

A short visit to the notable historic properties in Boreham, New Hall Y Boreham House, were then made, then on to the roadside memorial, where former pilot John Connelly from Oregon placed a wreath. The guard of Honour was provided by the Chelmsford branch of the Air Training Corps.

Finally to the airfield, acknowledged as the best preserved of all former American wartime air bases in Essex. The visitor were driven around the perimeter track and along part of the old main

Men from the 394th Bomb Group in front of a Bed and Breakfast. L to R: Bill Reagan, Joe Jackson, John Connelly, Frank Centino, Russell Blakely.

Tree planting in Boreham. L to R: Chairman of the Parish Council (holding tree), John Connelly, Joe Jackson, Duane Reagan (with shovel), Russell Blakely, Frank Centinino, unidentified.

Madingley - Cambridge.

The 737-400 which flew the group to Cherbourg from Stanstead.

Officials presiding in ceremony and flag raising near village of Touren-Bessin where memorial is near site of A-13 from which the 394th flew.

804th, 204th NFSq R.A.F.
A 9 LE MOLAY
10th TRG 67th PRG
A 10 CARENTAN
50th FG
A 11 St LAMBERT
474th FG
A 12 LIGNEROLLES
362nd FG
A 13 TOUR EN BESSIN
373rd FG 406th FG 394th BG
A 14 CRETTEVILLE
406th FG 358th FG
A 16 BRUCHEVILLE
36th FG
A 17 MEAUTIS
50th FG
A 18 St JEAN DE DAYE
A 19 LA VIEILLE
370th FG
A 20 LESSAY
323rd BG

394th noted on Maupertus Monument at the Cherbourg Air Field.

Plaque on Memorial near A-13. Bayeux

runway to the control tower. They were met by members of the Essex Police helicopter unit, who control this activity from the renovated wartime control tower. The Americans were presented with a set of photographs of the helicopter and a drinking mug suitable inscribed with the unit badge. Members were also given a ride in the helicopter.

Then a nostalgic view of the airfield, seen in the evening sunshine from the roof of the control tower. Photographs of the veterans were taken here with the flag of the United States fluttering in the breeze. This was the first time that their flag had flown from here in 48 years.

A reception was held in the dining room of Ford Motor Company Motorsport Centre, located at the airfield. The room was decorated with numerous American Flags, and a collection of wartime photographs, taken at the airfield, were on display.

During the reception, the chairman of the Parish Council, Mr. Peter McMillan, presented the visitors with copies of the village's history, and Mr. Bryan Jones presented copies of his book, "Wings and Wheels - The History of Boreham Airfield".

Mr. John Connelly, on behalf of the American visitors, presented to Mr. McMillan a framed document of appreciation, expressing to the Parish Council and villagers, their sincere thanks for the hospitality and welcome given to them. Taped music, by the Glenn Miller orchestra, was played during the reception, giving the occasion a little atmosphere of wartime day.

Amongst the village people in attendance was the Mayor of Chelmsford, Councilor David Pyman and the Mayoress. The Americans said they were overwhelmed with the reception they had been given.

On Sunday morning the visitors joined their comrades who had been visiting their old bases in the country, and attended a wreath laying ceremony at the American Military Cemetery at Madingley, Cambridge.

During the evening, all the Americans, together with numerous English guests, attended a farewell dinner given by the Marauder Historical Society held at the Colchester Leisure Centre. Music was provided by the Nick Ross Orchestra, playing Glenn Miller tunes.

On Monday, the American party left by air for their visit to France, where they looked at old air bases they used after leaving England in 1944.

394 BOMBARDMENT GROUP TOUR OF FRANCE

The most stirring part for the 394th in France was the dedication of the monument near Tour-en-Bessin which was located near the end of the runway of A-13 where the 394th operated from August 25 to September 18, 1944.

The group was honored by local dignitaries as well as a band from the French Army, and high ranking French Army and Air Force officers. The ceremony consisted of a wreath laying and the simultaneous raising of the colors of France and the USA.

Prior to and shortly after, the ceremony traffic along the busy highway in front of the memorial was stopped.

After this ceremony we were taken to the local church for a brief ritual honoring the 384th.

From there we were escorted to the Tour-en-Bessin town hall for a Vin d'Honeur and were treated royally with generous food and drink. Bottles of the historical calvidos were plentiful, with complete instructions offered on the best way to consume it!

I was personally honored by being asked to write in their town equivalent of a guest book.

It was particularly impressive be- cause other famous personalities have signed it also, such as Dwight I Eisenhower, General Omar Bradley Nancy Reagan and others.

One more than middle-aged man thanked me for leaving a badly dam- aged B-26 for him and his friends to play in after we moved from A-13.

After this memorable occasion, we sadly boarded the bus for our hotel in Bayeux.

Wreath laying at the Arc de Triomphe.

Window in church at St. Mere Eglise, famous for commemorating paratroopers.

Roadside memorial on perimeter of Boreham Airfield.

John Connelly, on the left, talking to the airfield historian Bryan Jones, about his book.

394th Bomb Group men on top of the control tower at Boreham. L to R: Russell Blakely, Frank Dentanino, Warren V. Bigelow, Joseph Jackson, John Connelly, Duane 'Wild Bill' Reagan.

Chelmsford Police helicopter.

394TH BOMBARDMENT GROUP RETURN TO BOREHAM
Bryan Jones

Six former members, together with their wives, returned to Boreham. Although not many in number, they were given a very warm welcome and greatly enjoyed themselves.

The reception was overwhelming they said. On arrival in the village, they visited the 'Queen's Head' pub for a taste again of English beer. They attended a memorial tree planting and visited the village church to see the American flag hanging in memory of those who died on missions flown from the airfield.

Entertainment was in the form of tea parties in the homes of village people, followed by a visit to the old airfield recognized as being the best preserved of any of the remaining 9th U.S.A.F. Air Bases.

A wreath laying ceremony was then carried out at the road side memorial. John Connally, a former pilot, laid the wreath at the memorial on behalf of the veterans.

Photographs were then taken on the roof of the control tower, now used by Essex Police as a control centre for their helicopter operations. Then a helicopter flight over the airfield, which was said to be one of the highlights of their return.

More refreshments in the Ford Motorsport centre, now based at the airfield and then a presentation of village history books to all visitors, including copies of 'Wings and Wheels - The History of Boreham Airfield', by the airfield's historian, Bryan Jones.

The veterans finally departed after a rather hectic day for their hotel in Chelmsford.

397th Bombardment Group

Squadrons: 596th, 597th, 598th, 599th

Brief WW II History

The 397th Bomb Group was activated on April 20, 1943 at Mac Dill Field, Tampa, Florida and assigned the Martin B-26 Marauder aircraft. Assigned to the Ninth Air Force 98th Bomb Wing. The group's aircraft were flown via Ascension Island to England in March 1944 from Hunter Field, Savannah, Georgia.

The group participated in operations preparatory to the Normandy invasion by attacking V-weapon sites, bridges, coastal defenses, marshalling yards, and airfields between April and June 1944.

The 397th hit strong points in France on D-Day, June 6, 1944, and assisted ground forces throughout the remainder of the Normandy campaign by bombing fuel dumps, defended areas, and other objectives.

The group engaged in bombardment of German forces in the region of St. Lo during the Allied breakthrough there in July.

After moving to the continent in August, the 397th struck enemy positions at St. Malo and Brest and bombed targets in the Rouen area as Allied armies swept across the Seine and advanced to the Siegfried Line.

In September, the group began flying missions into Germany, attacking bridges, defended areas and storage depots.

During the Battle of the Bulge (December 1944), the 397th struck the enemy's communications system and received the Distinguished Unit Citation for a mission on December 23 when the group withstood heavy flak and fighter attacks to sever a railway bridge at Eller, a vital link in the enemy's supply line across the Moselle. Ten losses.

The group continued to support the Allied drive into Germany until April 1945.

The 397th returned to the United States during December 1945 and January 1946, and was inactivated on January 6.

Group Staff, early 1944: Colonel Richard T. Coiner, Jr. (Commander); L/Col. Rollin M. Winingham (Deputy Cmdr.); Maj. Kenneth C. Dempster (Operations Officer); Capt. George D. Hughes (Asst. Ops. Officer); Maj. Franklin E. Ebeling (Exec. Officer); Maj. Kenneth R. Majors (Adjutant); Maj. Thomas E. McLeod (Intelligence Officer); Lt. Timberlake (Asst. Intell. Officer); Maj. Robert L. McCollum (Group Surgeon); Capt. William Rafkind (Communications); Capt. Joseph A. D'Andrea (Special Services); Capt. Clarence R. Comfort (Chaplain); Capt. Earl W. Udick (Group Navigator); Capt. William H. Bond (Group Bombardier); Capt. Elton G. Morrow (Maintenance Officer); Capt. Claude J. Funderburk (Supply Officer), Capt. Fred E. Seale, Jr. (Armamet Officer); Capt. James M. Lynch, Jr. (Controller); Lt. John F. Haupt, Jr. (Ordnance); Lt. Charles H. Schultz (Weather); Lt. Henry C. Beck, Jr. (Photo Interpreter); Lt. James M. Snow (Photo); Lt. Deane Weinberg, Jr. (Personnel). Squadron commanders: 596th, Maj. Robert M. McLeod; 597th, Maj. Frank L. Wood, Jr; 598th. Maj. Franklin S. Allen, Jr.; 599th, Maj. Eugene H. Berkenkamp.

THE RETURN OF RIVENHALL'S AMERICANS—THE 397TH BOMB GROUP

The Return to RAF Rivenhall near the villages of Revenhall and Silver End, Essex, England

A tremendous welcome awaited the veterans of the 397th Bombardment Group when they arrived at the village of Silver End on Saturday, May 2, 1992.

As the bus load of veterans arrived they were greeted by a flag waving, cheering crowd that appeared to be the entire population of the villages of Rivenhall and Silver End. Headmaster John Jemison of the local primary school, with a colorful headdress was the "chief cheer leader."

The airbase located between the two villages, was officially named, "RAF Rivenhall." The villagers of Silver End liked to call it, "Silver End'drome."

Chairman Pamela Bugg, Silver End Parish Council, gave a warm welcome address, which kicked off the festivities. George W. Parker, responded for the 397th and introduced Co-Chairman Chuck Slovachek (397th/598th) and Nevin Price, Secy/Treasurer of the 397th BG Association. The President of the 397th Association, Robert M. McLeod, sent best wishes on behalf of the Group. McLeod was Commander of the 596th Squadron at Rivenhall in 1944.

After an expression of gratitude for the warm welcome, Parker cited two examples of what had become of the young men of 1944 at Rivenhall. First mentioned was Brad Boyar, who had been in the RAF flying Beaufighters and had flown on escort missions for Mr. Churchill prior to joining the 397th. He completed some thirty years as an airline pilot. Brad and his wife Estella were introduced.

The second example mentioned was Russ Agneta, who had been an enlisted bombardier in the mid to late thirties prior to WW II. He came back in the Air Corps when WW II began and was in the 397th as a Sergeant bombardier. After the war, he became an aeronautical engineer and was project engineer on the moon vehicle while working for Republic Aviation Company on Long

It looked like the entire villages of Rivenhall and Silver End turned out to greet the 397th on May 2, 1992 at Silver End.

Brad Boyar of Dallas, Texas was remembered at the 397th welcom as one of the "old" men of the 397th. He was a pilot in the RAF before joining the 397th and had escorted Winston Churchill's plane while flying the British Beaufighter.

The 397th veterans, their spouses and guests were overwhelmed by the tremendous welcome. May 2, 1992 at Silver End.

Island, New York. Russ did not make this 1992 visit.

After the initial welcome, it was a short walk through the local park to the next stop at the Congregational Church Hall. Pastor Patrick Baxter welcomed the visitors here. An impressive honor guard organized with the Cadet Marshalls, lined the entrance. Steve Signorelli and Pilot Officer Simon Redican of the 158 Squadron Air Training Corps chaired the honor guard event.

Many local villagers were on hand to greet and visit with the 397th visitors. The reception and lunch with friendly people provided a good atmosphere for visiting. One end of the hall was filled with WW II pictures and memorabilia. In the back yard was an old fashion fair with booths.

Carol De Coverly, a local historian on the 397th, provided most of the WW II display. As the 397th veterans approached the display, Carol invited them to sign their names on a piece of metal lying on a table. It was marked as "093" and was about 12" x 30".

When George Parker approached the display, both he and De Coverly were surprised. It turns out Parker was the instructor pilot shooting landings with Lt. Steve Weatherby on 28 July 1944 using an aircraft from the pool of spares for the training flight. S/Sgt. Robert Mink was the only other crew member—a flight engineer/gunner.

On the third or fourth take off, with the nose wheel off the ground and the ship about ready to fly, the left main tire blew out. The left main gear collapsed immediately. The left engine's four bladed prop hit the runway and the engine was cartwheeled off to the left leaving gas lines broken. The plane was on fire by the time it stopped; the crew jumped out and ran away. A fire wagon reached the aircraft, but to no avail—it burned to the ground. (For pictures of B-26 #296093, see page 70 of the book by B.A. Stait entitled, Rivenhall—The History of an Essex Airfield; 1984, Alan Sutton Pub. Ltd., Gloucester, Great Britain.)

Next on the agenda was maypole dancing by the children in the park nearby. This was a good opportunity for the 397th visitors to meet and mingle with the children of all ages. At the park, Ken Millen of the Silver End Po-

Dinner at Silver End Hotel on May 2, 1992. L to R: Co-chairman, Chuck Slovachek; Mayor Kiernan Boylan; Co-chairman George Parker; Mrs. Boylan.

L to R: Jeremy White - general chairman for the event; Jack Mullin - flew the Marauder with the S. African Air Force on loan from the RAF; George Parker - 397th chairman for the visit to England; Anthony Newton - OBE, MP, Leader of the house of Commons.

The 397th dinner at the Silver End Hotel. L to R: Lois (Mrs. George) Parker - 397th Chairman; John Perks - Braintree District Cormeil; Joan Lyon - Essex County Counselor.

May 2, 1992 - Tree planting at the St. Mary's All Saints Church, Rivenhall. The tree planted was from the two Florida oaks planted on RAF Rivenhall by members of the 397th in 1944. L to R: Claude Hayes (with shovel), Sid Gurton and George Parker.

At the same time a tree planting ceremony took place at Rivenhall, a tree was being planted at Silver End. Both plantings came from two Florida oaks

lice contingent, presented a British policeman's hat, which Co-Chairmen of the 397th visit George Parker and Chuck Slovacheck, accepted and tried on for size—a perfect fit.

Next was a tree planting ceremony, which took place simultaneously at the Rivenhall St. Mary's All Saints Church and in the park at Silver End. Sprouts from a Florida Oak planted on the airbase in 1944 by Americans, were planted. Rev. Nigel Cooper of the Rivenhall Church gave the invocation there and Rev. Patrick Baxter at Silver End.

A bus trip to visit the airfield was one highlight of the day. The Marconi Company has used the airbase for the past several years conducting experiments with radar antennas. The old runway was still there—most of the buildings are gone. Chairman of the Silver End portion of the festivities, Phil Shute, served as the tour guide for the airfield visit. A pilot himself, and much younger than the B-26 veterans, Phil stirred emotions when he said he had landed recently at the field or had flown over it and while doing so, imagined himself flying a B-26 and wondered what it would have been like in 1944.

After a couple hours of free time visiting with the village people, it was off to the Silver End Hotel for the evening event billed as "1940s Music and Buffet." General Chairman Jeremy White of Silver End took charge. The 397th visitors consisted of forty (24 veterans & 16 wives). The total attendance at the dinner was about 150. A special friend of the B-26 Marauder Historical Society who attended, was Jack Mullin of Stalybridge, Cheshire, England. He was with an RAF B-26 crew in WW II, which was assigned to a South African B-26 Squadron in the Mediterranean area.

Several dignitaries welcomed the 397th at the dinner including: Essex County Counselor, Mrs. Joan Lyon; Mayor Kiernan Boylan of Witham, Chairman John Perks, Braintree District Council; Rt. Hon. Antony Newton, OBE,MP; Sid Gurton, Rivenhall Parish Council member filled in for Chairman Terry Lake; Chairman Pamela Bugg, Silver End Parish Council.

Chairman White was assisted by Phil Shute and Carol De Coverly in presenting a framed photo of the 397th flying over Essex in 1944. The inscription reads:

Presented by the people from the locality of Rivenhall Airfield in commemoration and gratitude for the 397th Bomb Group's service and sacrifice in the cause of freedom.

15th April - 5th August 1944
Presented 2nd May 1992

Co-Chairmen for the 397th, Parker and Slovachek, presented a B-26 model painted with the 397th markings and a framed print of a B-26. The inscriptions read:

To the people of Essex upon the Return of the Marauder Men, May 2, 1992, with gratitude.

397th Bomb Group Assoc.

R.A.F. Rivenhall Airfield; "Silver End'drome," 1944

Responding to the words of welcome, 397th spokesman Parker expressed appreciation for the wonderful day of renewed friendships and the hospitality and graciousness of the Rivenhall and Silver End people. "Under the circumstances of our visit to Essex in 1944 and considering our youthful age it seems to me that we have a feeling of roots for this place. Somehow, I believe that we have some roots at Rivenhall and Silver End,' he said.

"And," Parker continued, "I believe our good feeling about this place today has a great deal to do with the kindness of the people of Essex and something to do with one's love of their fellowman."

The music was great, the food was great, the spirit we found was great, the welcome received by the 397th was genuine and all this and more made this a very joyous occasion.

In addition to the names of people already mentioned, some leading roles were played by others, who worked on the planning or arrangements for this day: Rose and John Reader, Witham; Norman Sparrow, Braintree; Greta Tew, Silver End; Mike Selby, Rivenhall; Charlie Gardner, George and Jenny Phillips, Alan Gray, Ted Rothon, Richard Witney of Silver End.

Just before we departed, De Coverly stirred our emotions when he brought forth the flag from Guard Post #6 at RAF Rivenhall, which he had recovered when the airfield was closed. It had hung in his bedroom all these years. He wanted to preserve it in memory of the 397th whom he remembered as a small boy in 1944. Parker accepted it for the 397th.

Trying on the British policeman's hat which was presented by Ken Millen. L to R: Chuck Slovachek, Ken Millen and George Howard.

George Parker and Chuck Slovachek accept the gift photo for the 397th. L to R: Jeremy White, George Parker and Chuck Slovachek.

The 397th aircraft model presented by Chuck Slovachek and George Parker. L to R: Slovachek, Parker, Carol De Coverly and Jeremy White (hidden) accepting it.

L to R: Carol DeCoverly (397th History of Essex) and Phil Shute, Vice-Chairman for the 397th Return to Rivenhall - Silver End. The flag was from Guard Post #5 at RAF Rivenhall and DeCoverly recovered it when the base was closed after WW II.

397th veterans on the old runway at RAF Rivenhall. L to R: Fred King, Richard Atkinson, Claude Hays and Don Von Gal.

Return to Airfield A-26 at the Villages of Gorges and Gonfreville, Normandy, France

On May 5, the 397th bus arrived at the church at Gonfreville, Normandy, about 10:30 a.m.

Stopping in the town of Periers enroute to the Village of Gonfreville, the bus driver was not sure of the correct road to follow. A kind gentlemen driving by the bus saw a few fellas standing near the bus door and probably looking a bit lost. He stopped and asked if he could help. It turned out that he was on his way to Gonfreville to take part in the 397th visit. He lead us to Gonfreville. His name, Henri G. Levaufre.

Dignitaries on hand to meet the 397th bus included: Mayor Louis Brotelande of Gorges, Mayor Du Jardin of Gonfreville, President Beatrice Bouvier-Muller of the French-American Ninth Air Force Normandy Air-Fields Association, President Gustave Couillard, Para Club de la Manche; Bernard Boulanger, who had served with General Patton's 3rd Army LeClerc Division; Capitaine Daniel Lung, representing the French Air Force; Pierre Lecocq of Gorges and Jules Castelain. Castelain, in his French Army uniform, had served in the 3rd Army too and was the master of ceremonies for the 397th monument dedication.

The first part of the day's program was a special mass at the church. Special honor guards and color guards entered the church first. It was a colorful occasion and the crowd overflowed with several standing at the entrance.

Following the mass, the color guards, which included four U.S. Air Force members stationed in Germany (Denise L. Cormier, Christopher Esposito, Randy Nicely and Nanette R. Lofton), who had volunteered for the assignment, proceeded to lead the procession to the 397th monument scene.

The procession with the flag bearers, the dignitaries and the crowd, including children in colorful dress, was an impressive sight. It caused individuals to feel that something important was about the happen.

MC Jules Castgelain took charge in a dignified manner. The flag bearers lined up behind the veiled monument. Some 30 to 40 children were positioned on the left.

The 397th is welcomed at Gonfreville - May 5, 1992.

The procession moves toward the 397th monument to be dedicated in honor of the veterans of the 397th who worked and flew from the metal strip runway at Gorges/Gonfreville.

Getting in place at the 397th monument dedication at Gorges/Gonfreville.

Don Von Gal (397th BG), May 5, 1992 at the 397th monument at Gorges-Gonfreville.

397th veterans meet the VIP, May 5, 1992. L to R: Martin Fleisher, Nevin Price, Chuck Slovachek, George Parker, Jules Castelain and Madam Beatrice Bouvier-Muller. Castelain served as MC for the dedication ceremony.

Two 397th members were asked to raise the American flag on the pole to the right of the monument. Chuck Slovachek (397/598th) and Fred Ellinghaus (397/597th) raised the flag.

This was an especially emotional occasion for Ellinghaus in that he had discovered on this Return of the Marauder Men visit that one of his flight crew was buried in Europe. This was a surprise revelation to him.

The monument dedication proceeded. The unveiling revealed a brownish granite stone about five feet high with these words thereon:

NINTH USA AIR FORCE WWII
THE 397th BOMBARDMENT GROUP
FLEW FROM
THIS ADVANCED LANDING
GROUND A-26
BUILT BY
826th AVIATION ENGINEER BAT-
TALION 08.30 to 09.16.1944
IN RESPECTFUL MEMORY OF
THOSE
WHO GAVE THEIR LIVES FOR
LIBERTY

GORGES-GONFREVILLE
5 May 1992

Several speakers paid tribute and expressed gratitude for the 397th Marauder Men's service in World War II including Mayor Brotelande and Du Jardin of Gorges and Gonfreville respectively. Madam Beatrice Bouvier-Muller (Her son, Francois served as interpreter for the day).

Madam Beatrice Bouvier-Muller spoke at the dedication at Gorges/Gonfreville.

The children sang, "La Marseillaise." This caused some tears. The finale was three parachutists dropping with precision near the monument in a field of cattle: Michel Deshuelles, Jean Piedle and Andre Chauvin. Michel, we heard had made over 5,000 jumps and every year on the 6th of June he parachutes into Ste. Mere Eglise in tribute to fellow parachutists who landed there in the invasion of 1944, and we suspect, in memory of John Steel, who hung from the steeple all that night.

A special plaque for the 397th was presented by President Gustave Couillard of the Para Club de la Manche.

Fred King (397th/596th) was impressed when one of the Frenchmen at the dedication showed him the original typed permit for him to drive a truck for the 826th Aviation Engineer Battalion in building the airfield (A-26).

From the monument scene, the next event was a reception and lunch at Gorges. The informal visiting that took place on this occasion was a highlight of the day. At lunch, the Americans were scattered throughout the audience. It was an occasion filled with a friendly atmosphere. One 397th Marauder Man

Parachute club jumpers at the 397th monument dedication, May 5, 1992.

Mayor of Gonfreville Du Jardin receives the 397th plaque for the villages of Gorges and Gonfreville.

The three parachute jumpers at the 397th monument dedication are shown with Bernard Boulanger. L to R: Andre Chauvin, Jean Piedler, Bernard Boulanger and Michel Deshevlles.

The 397th veterans wave appreciation to the village folks of Gorges and Gonfreville.

said, "I wished we could have spent the whole day visiting with those nice people. They had so many interesting experiences about Normandy and 1944."

A sample of the stories which made the luncheon so enjoyable for the Americans: When a five year old boy in 1944, this Frenchman said he and several members of his family saw a crew parachute out of a B-26. The Germans came and found parachutes, searched all the surrounding houses, but did not find the aircrew hiding in the woods.

As a boy, he said he remembered his father taking food and milk into the woods late at night to feed the Americans. Within a week, the French underground helped the crew escape.

George Parker and Chuck Slovachek, Co-Chairmen for the 397th visit, presented a 397th plaque to the Mayors of Gorges and Gonfreville.

After the delightful lunch, that ended about 3 p.m., the next bus stop was at Ste. Mere Eglise where a stuffed paratrooper still hangs from the local cathedral. A brief stop at the airborne museum there then back to the bus. Next stop—Omaha Beach and the Normandy American Cemetery.

On the way out of the cemetery, three of the 397th men struck up a conversation with a man about the surroundings. When the fellow found out that they were B-26 crewmen, he told how a B-26 crew had recently been identified after being listed as missing in action since 6 June 1944.

A French farmer was plowing his field when he came upon some parts of an airplane, then remains of bodies. He notified the authorities. It took a long time, perhaps two or three years to make positive identification. He said it turned out to be a squadron commander and his entire crew, seven men total. They had been shot down on D-Day and had been missing nearly fifty years.

The fellow relating this story turned out to be the Superintendent of the Cemetery. He said the missing crew was from the 386th Bomb Group. He gave us a list of the crew, which we passed on to one of the leaders of the 386th Bomb Group Association.

The 397th's return to Gorges and Gonfreville was a wonderful occasion. We cannot adequately explain the feelings, the emotions that came upon us under these circumstances. The people of Normandy, and especially the people of Gorges and Gonfreville, are very special people who have seen and endured war.

It seems we Americans who were there in 1944 have a close kinship with them and it was a joy to be with them again nearly fifty years later.

TWIN ORPHANS

Tucking in a meal which included fried eggs and bacon, tasting ice cream and stuffing ourselves with chocolate and even chewing gum, this was a rare treat.

My twin brother, Donald, and I were among a group of six happy children, being entertained on an Air Base in 1944 during the war.

There were rides on a Jeep and the thrill of climbing into the cockpit of a B-26 Bomber. I was fascinated when I saw a typewriter for the very first time and felt quite proud when invited to try it out. We left the Air Base loaded with toys, sweets and lots of souvenirs - some of which I still have. A truly marvelous day. I remember off-loading my over indulgence in the chauffeur driven car on the homeward journey, much to everyone's disgust.

The six orphaned children were guests of the B-26 Marauder Wing of the U.S. Air Force, at the Riverhall Air Base. We had all been "adopted" by this Unit through a "Five Year Plan" which through their generosity provided extra food, clothes and holidays, as well at 20 lira per year. "Providing the jam for the bread" as it was called. Some of this money was in the form of Savings Certificates, which turned up out of the blue in 1968.

My dad died in North Africa in December 1943. He was in the 8th Army Desert Rats. My mother was left with five children to bring —not very easy. In fact, I don't know how she coped. War widows have always been overlooked. I remember the food parcels from the American Red Cross who came to our aid and gave us most support. They were very welcome.

We were evacuated at the outbreak of the war in 1940 to Devon, in the West country. Later we spent a couple of years in Wales where Donald and I went to the School — that wasn't too bad — in fact we had an enjoyable time, getting up to a lot of mischief, probably. We still had regular contact with Mrs. Honeyball (our evacuee mother), "Ma", as we called her, up to a few years ago when she died.

In 1945, I remember the dreaded Buzz Bombs, falling over London. The memory of which will stay with me forever. My mum was bombed out at least once.

I often look at the photographs of our marvelous day on the air base, with our "American Uncles" and although we lost contact after the war, I used to wonder what happened to them—what had life in store for them all — what became of the other orphans?

Sadly, my brother Donald, died in 1978 at the age of 44 years. leaving a wife and eight children, jokingly he used to say that he wanted a football team — most of his family are now grown up with families of their own. Phyllis and I have no children, "C'est la Vie".

The Sunday Express Newspaper helped to bring about a wonderful reunion in 1984, when the 397th Marauder Group came to Europe, for the 40th Anniversary of the D-Day landings. They wanted to meet the orphans once again and on June 12th, 1984, after the Express managed to trace all but one of the children, Joanne Smith, who accompanied by her husband and Phyllis and myself, were invited to their reunion dinner at the Gloucester Hotel, here in London. There were so many familiar faces from so long ago, a very enjoyable evening. It was so nice to meet with Joanne again.

There was a nostalgic trip to the Rivenhall Air Base. The Directors of Marconi Systems kindly allowed us to look around. The runways are mostly overgrown now, the hangers empty and silent. Some of the Nissen huts are still standing, including the canteen which is in daily use. The site is shortly to be bull-dozed for redevelopment. Finally, there was a visit to the War Memorial at Mattingley for a short service.

In October, 1985, Phyllis and I were invited to the group's reunion in San Diego. We had a fabulous time and in September we are off again to Dayton, Ohio. I can never find the words to express our heartfelt thanks and appreciation of our continued friendship with 397th Bomber Group.

Nick Chacos, 397th member, stands in front of sign designating the village where he was housed during the conflict in WW II.

Report On "The Return Of The Maraudermen"
April 28 to May 8, 1992
Eight B-26 Groups Represented

Erwin J. Cook

April 30, 1992, Thursday

After overnight flight, arrived in London. We were met at the airport by a number of the press. Interviews took place while waiting for others to be processed by customs. Transferred to hotel, "Kensington Close." Since my wife Barbara was not along, a TV crew asked me to spend the afternoon in London showing them places that had a special meaning in 1944.

The first place we hit was Selfridges Department Store, where Marvin Schulze and I always went for a waffle when in London. Then on to Piccadilly Circus and the Regent Palace Hotel where we occasionally stayed. Then to SOHO to remember "The Mill Theatre," popular with the troops.

Next stop was "The War Museum," where I presented "Captain Marvin Schulze's Personal Diary," which was videoed by the TV crew. The names of the crew were given in the discussion of this copy of his diary.

The TV crew and I then went back to Piccadilly Circus for them to tape a discussion of the Buzz Bomb, with the traffic as a background. At 6:30 p.m. we called it quits and I collapsed into bed.

May 1, Friday

Short city tour of London on our way to the Harlequin Hotel at Stansted where we are to stay three nights. That evening there was a reception at the Essex County Hall in Chelmsford. It was a large multi-story building which was packed. Several speeches with an exchange of mementos. The police band was excellent, playing some 40s tunes. After food had been served, a local dance group entertained us.

Frank Brewer (323rd Group) President of the "Marauder Historical Society" represented the total of all groups when we were all together. George Parker and Chuck Slovachek represented the 397th when only our group was at an event. I counted 18 — 397th men, some with wives, on the trip.

The entrance to the main dining room at the Harlequin Hotel, May 1, 1992.

397th Marauder men arrive at Silver End on May 2, 1992. George Parker responded to the welcome by Parish Council Chairman Pamela Bugg of Silver End.

May 2, Saturday

The entire group went to Duxford Imperial War Museum to see the exhibits. The Eighth Air Force has an excellent exhibit here. Harvey Beck's picture board of the 397th group was there and very much appreciated. Five of the greeters were dressed in American WW II uniforms. The RAF Marauders Association joined us for lunch at the Officers Club.

In the p.m. the groups broke up to go to their various villages where they had been stationed in 1944. The 397th visited Silver End and Rivenhall. First there was a huge greeting by the villagers in front of the Silver End Hotel. Some

short speeches with much flag waving and expressions of welcome, with a response by George Parker and Chuck Slovachek.

Then a short walk through the cherry trees in the park to the congregational church. There was a display of pictures and mementos of the WW II era, including the 397th. In the back yard was an old-fashioned fair with booths. Lunch was served. A tree was planted in the church yard to commemorate our visit. We were on our own for a couple of hours to visit with the locals. About 5 p.m. we started gathering in the pub to be ready for the dinner and dance to follow. The evening started with a glass of wine, followed by dinner. George Parker and Chuck Slovachek represented the 397th as co-chairman at this event. There were presentations from both sides of mementos, greeting and thank yous.

At 10 p.m. as we left Silver End Hotel by bus, we could see a huge fireworks display in the distance. We realized that it was probably seen by all of the groups too as they left their villages.

May 3, Sunday

A beautiful, sunny day to visit Madingley U.S. Military Cemetery. There was a beautiful, emotional ceremony to honor those that had died. Each group laid a wreath. If I understood correctly, there are about 90 B-26 people buried here. After the fly over, we returned to the Harlequin Hotel. A word about the hotel. They had really gotten into this trip by dressing the desk clerks in WW II uniforms; also had streamers of British and American flags. In the lobby were stacks of sandbags similar to WW II. The front of the restaurant looked like the end of a quonset hut, with a sign P-X. Incidentally, the food was top drawer.

That evening everyone was collected up for an evening at the Colchester Leisure Centre in Colchester. A buffet dinner was served, along with Glenn Miller music with a dance. The speaker was Roger Freeman who put together the recent book, "B-26 Marauder at War." A fun evening.

May 4, Monday

Flight from Stansted Airport to Cherbourg Maudertus Airport. We are joined here by the French Marauders Association. There was a ceremony here to honor those Americans who had died in the freeing of France. The display of the flags and banners was very impressive. Short speeches by the French and Americans. A reception was held in a hall in Cherbourg.

Next stop Lessay Airfield for lunch where a large crowd awaited. There was a special dedication here for the 323rd group, which was Frank Brewer's group. The folks were very warm and cordial, giving us samples of their cheese and wine to take with us. Weather is great. Stopped in St. Mere Eglise to see the parachutist display on the church.

May 5, Tuesday

Headed for Gorges/Gonfreville area for a commemoration of our stop here (397th) in 1944. We flew five missions here off steel mats located in an apple orchard. Two of the adults, who were teenagers in 1944, told about playing in one of our crashed and abandoned ships after we left.

The ceremony started with a mass at the church located next to the past airfield which is long gone. The steel mats were taken up to make pigpens, some still in use.

We then moved down the road to about where the center of the runway would have been. Here a granite marker has been erected by the side of the road, honoring the 397th for their role in WW II.

We then went to a center in Gorges to have dinner with the locals. Some problems with the language barrier, but we did manage to communicate. Each 397th man was expected to sit with a local family. As the wine flowed, the communication improved. What wonderful, warm people. Many thank yous for our being there in 1944. Just before we left, out came the calvados. That just about finished us off.

Then the next stop was Omaha Beach, which has been left as it was during the war. The 397th bombed gun emplacements north of here on Mission No. 2 on D-Day. On our way back to the hotel we stopped at Normandy American Cemetery. In 1988, they told about a farmer digging up pieces of a B-26. The authorities dug it up and were able to identify the missing-in-action crew. The pilot and co-pilot were Lt. Colonels. I believe they were from the 386th Bomb Group, but my memory may be faulty.

May 6, Wednesday

On to Paris for a visit to the Main City Hall of Paris, for the reception. What a beautiful building. It was furnished better than some palaces I've seen. The ceremony focused on all B-26 units, including the French.

Next item on the itinerary was a visit to the Arc de Triomphe to relight the eternal flame in commemoration of those who had died in the two world wars. The ceremony started with a short march up the Champs Elysées to the Arc. Then the symbolic relighting ceremony, after which we all signed the book kept at the Arc de Triomphe.

After the overnight stay in Paris, the bus drove to Calais for the ferry trip to Dover. The highlight of this part of the trip was Leeds Castle. It is set on two small islands in 500 acres of park land. It is kept up so it can be used for conferences and tourist dinners. It is described as a fairy tale medieval fortress, which it certainly is. Turned out to be a perfect warm day, which contributed to the enjoyment.

Stayed in a lovely hotel near Heathrow for return to the states on May 8, 1992.

Others extended their stay before and after "The Return of the Maraudermen" tour.

I counted about 280 people total on this tour. There were fewer on the France segment.

It was absolutely a fantastic trip. Thanks for all that were in on the planning and doing.

The 397th reception in the church hall, Silver End.

ARDENNES CEMETERY

Ardennes Cemetery is located near the southeast edge of Neupre (Newville-en-Condroz), 12 miles southwest of Liege, Belgium.

The approach drive leads to the memorial, a rectangular stone structure bearing on its facade a massive American eagle and other symbolical sculpture. Within are the chapel, three large wall maps composed of inlaid marbles, marble panels depicting combat and supply activities and other ornamental features. Along the outside of the memorial, inscribed on granite slabs, are the names of 462 of the Missing who gave their lives in the service of their Country, but whose remains were never recovered or identified. The facade on the far (north) end which overlooks the burial area bears the insignia, in mosaic, of the major United States units which operated in Northwest Europe in World War II.

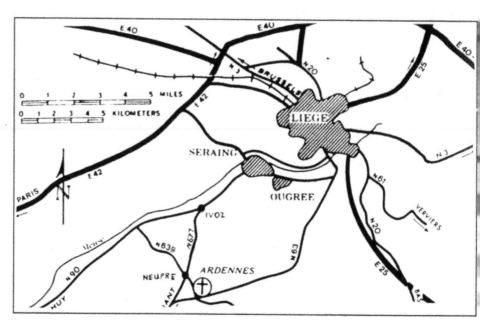

The cemetery, 90 acres in extent, contains the graves of 5,328 of our military Dead, many of whom died in the so-called "Battle of the Bulge." Their headstones are aligned in straight rows which compose the form of a huge Greek cross on the lawns and are enframed by tree masses.

HISTORY

Patrols of the U.S. First Army crossed the German frontier in the Ardennes area on 11 September and the next day crossed the German frontier near Aachen. Moving eastward toward the Siegfried Line, they quickly encountered strong resistance. Almost simultaneously progress slowed all along the advancing Allied line as opposition stiffened. The retreating enemy finally had achieved a stabilized defensive line.

After the bold but unsuccessful airborne effort to establish crossings of the lower Rhine in late September, the main effort of the Allies was shifted to the center where the U.S. Ninth Air Force, encircled Aachen which surrendered on 21 October. The U.S. Ninth Army, organized at Brest in Brittany, was shifted early in November from the right of the U.S. First Army to its left. Together they continued the attack to the Roer River against bitter opposition, especially in the dense Hurtgen Forest.

The Allied attacks were suddenly interrupted in the Ardennes on 16 December, when the enemy launched against the U.S. First and Third Armies its final major counteroffensive of the war. Popularly known as the "Battle of the Bulge," it was officially designated the Ardennes-Alsace Campaign which included the second half of the enemy's planned counteroffensive that was launched on New Year's Eve in Alsace to the south against the U.S. Seventh Army and the French First Army. After furious struggles in bitterly cold weather, all of the attacks were halted.

As the enemy onslaughts in the Ardennes and Alsace were being brought to a halt, plans were being prepared and approved by the Allies establishing three major successive objectives: the destruction of enemy forces west of the Rhine, the seizure of bridgeheads across the river, then coordinated drives into the heart of German. The first phase commenced with an advance on 2 February 1945 by the U.S. First Army in the center to seize control of the upstream dams on the Roer River. In the north, the advance to the Rhine was to begin on 8 February with the Canadian First Army advancing to the southeast, to be followed two days later with a converging attack to the northeast by the U.S. Ninth Army. But on 10 February when the U.S. First Army reached the last and most important dam, it was discovered that the enemy had wrecked the discharge valves during the previous night. The resultant heavy flow of water from the dams halted the U.S. Ninth Army on the north for two weeks.

On 23 February, the U.S. Ninth Army began its crossing of the Roer and the U.S. First Army renewed its advance to the Rhine. As the offensive gained momentum, it became a pursuit to destroy as many enemy units as possible before they could cross the Rhine. The U.S. First Army reached Cologne on 5 March; two days later it seized the only undemolished bridge across the Rhine which was located at Remagen. By 10 March, the entire west bank of the Rhine was in Allied hands.

The unanticipated good fortune was exploited immediately. Additional troops were rushed to the area. By 21 March the bridgehead was expanded to a width of 20 miles and a depth of eight miles. the next day, 22 March, the U.S. Third Army made a surprise amphibious crossing of the Rhine at Oppenheim. On 23 and 24 March, the long-planned major amphibious and airborne assault crossing of the Rhine by the British Second, the Canadian First and the U.S. Ninth Armies was carried out. Then in rapid succession, the U.S. First and Third Armies broke out of their bridgeheads on 25 March, the U.S. Seventh Army crossed the Rhine near Worms on 26 March and the French First Army crossed it on 31 March, thus achieving the first two planned objectives. Four days later the encirclement of the Ruhr Valley was completed as all Allied Armies continued to advance into German on a broad front.

Graves Area and North Facade of Chapel — Ardennes American Cemetery and Memorial.

ARDENNES CEMETERY

Name & Rank	Unit	Gp	Pl-Row-Gr	Number	Date of Death	Cemetery
GROTENHUIS, JOHN PFC	451BS	322	D-32-9	16084821	13 OCT 44	ARDENNES
HADE, SAMUEL SGT	451BS	322	D-23-19	19061970	13 OCT 44	ARDENNES
JEFFERIES, EDWARD F. JR. 1/LT	450BS	322	C-34-1	0-791596	17 MAY 43	ARDENNES
JENNINGS, WAYNE L. S/SGT	450BS	322	B-40-44	36181527	22 FEB 45	ARDENNES
LOGAN, JAMES R. S/SGT	450BS	322	D-1-34	38233559	22 FEB 45	ARDENNES
MOSSMAN, JAMES B 1/LT	450BS	322	B-40-36	0-411064	22 FEB 45	ARDENNES
REHMI, LOUIS F. S/SGT	450BS	322	B-26-17	12077939	22 FEB 45	ARDENNES
REZABEK, FRANCIS F. MAJ	452BS	322	C-25-7	0-380116	23 NOV 43	ARDENNES
ROBERTSON, HERBERT S. S/SGT	451BS	322	B-38-19	18061933	13 OCT 44	ARDENNES
SMITH, JAY B. LT/COL	450BS	322	B-40-32	0-424144	22 FEB 45	ARDENNES
STEFFEN, ROBERT P. T/SGT	450BS	322	D-37-4	36207782	17 MAY 43	ARDENNES
SURRATT, RICHARD L. S/SGT	452BS	322	C-37-17	15112278	09 NOV 44	ARDENNES
TERHUNE, WILLIAM A. T/SGT	452BS	322	C-13-40	35041062	23 NOV 43	ARDENNES
THIBEAULT, GRANT H. CAPT	450BS	322	D-26-4	0-725921	22 FEB 45	ARDENNES
STROMAN, WILLIAM 2/LT	454BS	322	D-7-53	0-833440	25 MAR 45	ARDENNES
ASHBURN, JOSEPH R. S/SGT	454BS	323	C-14-27	39252676	18 APR 44	ARDENNES
BYERS, ELLIS S. 1/LT	454BS	323	B-18-12	0-672029	14 FEB 45	ARDENNES
ESTEL, FOREST F. T/SGT	453BS	323	B-29-2	33105396	25 MAY 44	ARDENNES
FORTWENGLER, WILLIAM T/SGT	456BS	323	B-11-8	35112464	03 NOV 43	ARDENNES
MABRY, JAMES M. FLT/O	456BS	323	A-31-41	T-124981	03 APR 45	ARDENNES
MOORE, JOHN E. SGT	454BS	323	C-13-36	51402180	18 APR 44	ARDENNES
SCHNELLER, FRIEDEL R. S/SGT	454BS	323	D-5-52	1308891	25 MAR 45	ARDENNES
YOSICK, JEROME S. 1/LT	453BS	323	B-43-1	0-821391	14 JAN 45	ARDENNES
ANDREWS, RICHARD C. 1/LT	495BS	344	B-24-15	0-731725	11 MAY 44	ARDENNES
BROOKER, CHARLES F. S/SGT	495BS	344	D-19-21	35516194	24 FEB 45	ARDENNES
COYASO, CRUZ SGT	497BS	344	C-33-5	39276672	13 FEB 45	ARDENNES
ERICKSON, JOHN G. S/SGT	497BS	344	B-44-48	31190967	10 MAY 44	ARDENNES
FITCH, RALPH H. T/SGT	497BS	344	D-32-13	11122096	10 MAY 44	ARDENNES
HEIST, WALTER H. SGT	496BS	344	C-14-25	32380856	27 APR 44	ARDENNES
MAETIN, WAYNE L. S/SGT	494BS	344	A-24-10	36566120	23 SEPT 44	ARDENNES
MORRISON, FREDERIC M. 1/LT	497BS	344	D-30-3	0-672172	10 MAY 44	ARDENNES
SADULA, EDWARD A. 2/LT	495BS	344	C-17-18	0-765728	06 OCT 44	ARDENNES
SHEEHAN, JOHN J. 1/LT	497BS	344	C-9-31	0-816603	23 FEB 45	ARDENNES
TEAGUE, SAMMIE E. JR. FLT/O	494BS	344	D-4-44	T-133477	13 MAY 45	ARDENNES
TRAUX, NORMAN H. S/SGT	495BS	344	B-43-11	37472042	06 OCT 44	ARDENNES
VAN BLARGAN, IRVIN F. SGT	494BS	344	B-39-44	33830134	13 MAY 45	ARDENNES
VAN OVER, THOMAS L. 1/LT	495BS	344	B-36-53	0-791742	24 FEB 45	ARDENNES
VANDER LUGT, CORNELIUS S/SGT	495BS	344	D-6-14	36460204	10 FEB 45	ARDENNES
WHITEHEAD, CLYDE T. 2/LT	494BS	344	B-39-57	0-696928	13 MAY 45	ARDENNES
BEEGLE, ROBERT R. S/SGT	555BS	386	D-36-17	33102012	18 NOV 44	ARDENNES

Name & Rank	Unit	Gp	Pl-Row-Gr	Number	Date of Death	Cemetery
FERRI, FRANK L. T/SGT	553BS	386	B-44-32	32452004	10 OCT 44	ARDENNES
HOPPE, HENRY S/SGT	553BS	386	B-17-13	32288960	29 MAY 44	ARDENNES
JACKSON, CHARLES A. 1/LT	555BS	386	A-12-18	0-732848	23 DEC 43	ARDENNES
KAY, FRANK J. 1/LT	554BS	386	A-21-1	0-696466	14 MAR 45	ARDENNES
MADISON, THOMAS L. T/SGT	554BS	385	D-1-36	39565418	14 MAR 45	ARDENNES
McINTIRE, MERLE B. FLT/O	554BS	386	C-14-50	T-062201	31 JUL 44	ARDENNES
McMULLEN, RAYMOND A. 1/LT	554BS	386	D-1-26	0-816525	14 MAR 45	ARDENNES
SMITH, WALTER A. S/SGT	554BS	386	C-13-43	16043745	31 JUL 44	ARDENNES
WHITE, LEONARD P. SGT	554BS	386	D-2-22	16076750	14 MAR 45	ARDENNES
BUSCH, FREDERICK J. 1/LT	558BS	387	A-14-19	0-798742	12 APR 44	ARDENNES
HINDMAN, MELBOURNE D. S/SGT	558BS	387	A-39-27	19073965	25 FEB 44	ARDENNES
LE BOEUF, JOHN M. J. 1/LT	HQ	387	B-31-6	0-707943	02 MAR 45	ARDENNES
MILLER, LEWIS C. SGT	558BS	387	D-6-4	35657297	06 DEC 44	ARDENNES
STAFFORD, HAROLD V. S/SGT	556BS	387	D-23-12	38495228	20 MAY 45	ARDENNES
WINSOR, ALEXANDER JR. 1/LT	558BS	387	B-30-17	0-688888	06 DEC 44	ARDENNES
JOHNSON, CLARK G. 2/LT	574BS	391	D-31-12	0-555011	03 APR 45	ARDENNES
LUNSFORD, ARTHUR M. SGT	574BS	391	D-33-13	34774196	03 APR 45	ARDENNES
McMAHON, WILLIAM J. SGT	574 BS	391	D-31-16	35146993	03 APR 45	ARDENNES
MOONEY, IRA L. T/SGT	573BS	391	C-7-9	13044644	23 DEC 44	ARDENNES
STEVENSON, WILBUR P. 1/LT	574BS	391	B-35-57	0-704857	23 DEV 44	ARDENNES
AMPOLOS, WILLIAM J. SGT	585BS	394	A-31-24	11119736	21 FEB 45	ARDENNES
HALE, ROBERT A. CAPT	585BS	394	B-43-46	0-423805	21 FEB 45	ARDENNES
WOODWORTH, DONALD B. 2/LT	585BS	394	B-43-45	0-721894	21 FEB 45	ARDENNES
LEWIS, CRAIG E. 1/LT	596BS	397	C-9-22	0-417548	23 DEC 44	ARDENNES

The memorial at the Ardennes Cemetery. This facade features a massive American eagle and other symbolical sculpture.

BRITTANY CEMETERY

Brittany Cemetery lies 1 1/2 miles southeast of the village of St. James (Manche), France 12 miles south of Avranches and 14 miles north of Fougeres.

At this cemetery, covering 28 acres of rolling from country near the eastern edge of Brittany, rest 4,410 of our Dead, most of whom gave their lives in the Normandy and Brittany campaigns in 1944. Along the retaining wall of the memorial terrace are inscribed the names of 498 of the Missing whose resting place "is known only to God."

The gray granite memorial, containing the chapel as well as two large operations maps with narratives and flags of our military services, overlooks the burial area. Interesting stained-glass and sculpture aid in embellishing the structure. The lookout platform of the tower, reached by 98 steps, affords a view of the stately pattern of the headstones, as well as of the peaceful surrounding countryside stretching northward to the sea and Mont St. Michel.

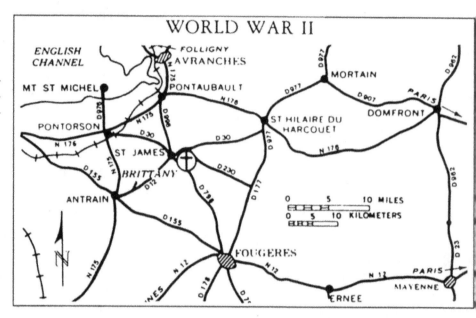

HISTORY

Ground combat in northwestern France commenced with the Allied landings on the beaches of Normandy, 6 June 1944. Under the cover of continuous naval gunfire and air support, the landings first objective, to link together the individual beachheads, was accomplished within a week. During the same period, temporary anchorage's and artificial harbors were created off the beachhead area by sinking ships and anchoring prefabricated concrete caissons to the channel floor, to facilitate the unloading of troops and supplies. As a result, the Allies were able to reinforce and increase the size and strength of their armies rapidly. The second objective of the landings was to clear the Cotentin Peninsula with its port of Cherbourg and capture Caen and St. Lo. On 26 June, American troops freed Cherbourg; 13 days later on 9 July, British and Canadian troops fought their way into Caen; and 18 July 1944, American troops took St. Lo, accomplishing the second objective. The final objective was to break through the ring of defenses that the enemy had established around the beaches. The stage was set for the breakout with a paralyzing air bombardment on 25 July by the U.S. Eighth and Ninth Air Forces and the Royal Air Force along a five

mile front west of St. Lo. Aided by British forces pinning down the enemy in the eastern portion of the beach area toward Caen, the U.S. First Army stormed out of the beachhead liberating Coutances three days later. Within a week, the newly activated U.S. Third Army had cleared Avranches and was advancing toward Paris on a broad front with the U.S. First Army. The two armies fanned our westward toward Brest, southward toward the Loire and eastward toward the Seine. On 7 August 1944, one week after the opening of the Avranches gap, a powerful counterattack was launched by the enemy, in an attempt to cut the columns of the advancing U.S. First and Third Armies. After the enemy's initial success in the region of Mortain, the U.W. First Army was able to stem the counterattack and push back enemy forces.

In mid-August, enemy forces were threatened with encirclement by the U.S. Third Army, which had turned northward from Le Mans, to meet the Canadian Army advancing southward from its beachhead. Despite desperate resistance by the enemy to prevent encirclement, the two Allied armies met at Chambois on 21 August. Enemy forces had the choice of remaining in the Falaise pocket or fleeing toward the Seine River in disorder. In a matter of days, U.S. Third Army troops were in the outskirts of Paris, liberating the city on 25 August 1944.

While these actions were taking place,

Cenotaph at East End of Mall — Brittany American Cemetery and Memorial.

the newly formed U.S. Ninth Army relieved the U.S. Third Army units that had remained in Brittany and took over their mission of containing the strong enemy garrisons which still held out there. Although stubbornly contested, St. Malo fell to U.S. forces on 1 September and Brest on 18 September 1944. At this time, most of the U.S. Ninth Army was ordered to the German border where enemy resistance was stiffening. Some U.S. Ninth Army units remained to contain the enemy garrisons at Lorient and St. Nazaire which did not surrender until 10 and 11 May 1945, respectively.

Brittany Cemetery with the memorial overlooking the burial area.

Youth Triumphing over Evil — Brittany American Cemetery and Memorial.

BRITTANY CEMETERY

Name & Rank	Unit	Gp	Pl-Row-Gr	Number	Date of Death	Cemetery
ABADY, CHARLES I. S/SGT	450BS	322	K-18-8	32874879	19 JUL 44	BRITTANY
BURNS, JAMES J. 1/LT	451BS	322	O-4-5	0-673217	19 JULY 44	BRITTANY
DEEN, JOY M. 1/LT	450BS	322	K-18-4	0-790806	19 JUL 44	BRITTANY
HEHL, RALPH V. SGT	451BS	322	L-11-14	35650495	19 JUL 44	BRITTANY
SIMPSON, JOHN G. COL	HQ	322	L-12-14	0-022869	20 JUL 44	BRITTANY
SINN, CARL H. 2/LT	450BS	322	K-14-19	0-761260	19 JUL 44	BRITTANY
WILLIAMS, JOHN F. T/SGT	450BS	322	K-7-9	39313446	19 JUL 44	BRITTANY
BRENAN, ALBERT G. T/SGT	455BS	323	P-1-20	06979275	06 JUN 44	BRITTANY
GILENO, GUIDO F. 2/LT	455BS	323	C-3-10	0-747005	06 JUN 44	BRITTANY
HARDY, LEONARD R. T/SGT	454BS	323	B-6-12	39682373	28 SEPT 44	BRITTANY
HAWKINSON, FRANK L. 1/LT	454BS	323	B-14-12	0-734911	28 SEPT 44	BRITTANY
MAXWELL, JOSEPH W. S/SGT	454BS	323	B-9-8	32470535	28 SEPT 44	BRITTANY
WATSON, WILLARD L. 2/LT	454BS	323	I-18-11	0-777878	28 SEPT 44	BRITTANY
MURRAY, EDWARD B. S/SGT	555BS	386	F-4-2	13108546	18 JUL 44	BRITTANY
ANNETTE, EDWARD J. T/SGT	573BS	391	F-1-1	32304424	25 AUG 44	BRITTANY
MEYER, ROY H. S/SGT	573BS	391	J-13-6	18192313	25 AUG 44	BRITTANY
THORN, DAVID H. CAPT	573BS	391	K-13-20	0-793198	25 AUG 44	BRITTANY
THOMAS, ARTHUR L. 1/LT	573BS	391	P-2-16	0-693957	25 AUG 44	BRITTANY
DAMER, DONALD B. 1/LT	587BS	394	N-4-19	0-816255	13 JUN 44	BRITTANY
ELYEA, CHARLES R. S/SGT	584BS	394	P-2-4	37550129	08 OCT 44	BRITTANY
HEMETER, VAN B. S/SGT	585BS	394	J-11-11	34624898	09 AUG 44	BRITTANY
NIELSEN, WILLIAM R. 2/LT	587BS	394	N-4-12	0-448316	13 JUN 44	BRITTANY
NIX, WILLIAM L. S/SGT	585BS	394	I-12-16	36485253	09 AUG 44	BRITTANY
STOLL, MILTON P. S/SGT	585BS	394	I-10-16	37662417	09 AUG 44	BRITTANY
WEST, JOHN Q. JR. CAPT	598BS	397	P-4-17	0-413177	01 AUG 44	BRITTANY

CAMBRIDGE CEMETERY

Cambridge Cemetery is situated 3 miles west of the university city of Cambridge, England, on highway A-1303 and 60 miles north of London.

The site, 301/2 acres in extent, was donated by the University of Cambridge. It lies on a north slope with wide prospect; the west and south sides are framed by woodland. The cemetery contains the remains of 3,812 of our military Dead; on the great Wall of the Missing are recorded the names of 5,126 who gave their lives in the service of their County, but who remains were never recovered or identified. Most of these died in the Battle of the Atlantic or in the strategic air bombardment of northwest Europe.

From the flagpole platform near the main entrance, the great mall and its reflecting pools stretch eastward, it is from this mall that the wide, sweeping curve of the burial area across the green lawns is best appreciated. Along the south side is the Wall of the Missing; at the far end is the memorial with its chapel, its two huge military maps, its stained-glass windows bearing the State Seals and military decorations and its mosaic ceiling memorial to the Dead of our Air Forces.

HISTORY

When the United States entered World War II, it was apparent that Germany; with its great military and industrial strength, posed the strongest threat of the Axis powers and should be dealt with first. Its defeat hinged on achieving four major objectives, Great Britain became a vast supply depot, military base, air base and training and staging facility. During the war, more than 17 million tons of cargo and nearly two million servicemen and women from the Untied States passed through British ports. Many military bases and training areas were established throughout the British Isles to receive the forces which later were to achieve such spectacular results on the beaches of Normandy. At the same time, airfields were enlarged and additional bases constructed for use by U.S. Army Air Forces.

The first objective in the war against Germany was to provide the United Kingdom with the resources needed to carry on until sufficient men, materials and supplies could be assembled for a cross-channel invasion of Europe. To do so, the Atlantic sea lanes had to be made safe for the passage of Allied convoys between Great Britain and the United States. The battle for the Atlantic continued from 1939 to 1945, when the last German U-boats surrendered. This costly, but generally successful struggle, gave the Allies control of the sea lanes between the United States and Great Britain, which was essential to the success of Allied operations in Europe.

The second objective was to aid and sustain other nations actively engaged against the Axis, particularly the U.S.S.R., which at the time was receiving the brunt of the enemy's land assaults. A "second front" was opened in North Africa in November 1942 to relieve the pressure against the U.S.S.R. Allied forces from bases in both Great Britain and the United States landed in North Africa and fought their way inland in the face of determined enemy resistance. Six months later, victory in North Africa was achieved when all enemy forces there surrendered. The operations in North Africa were followed by Allied landings in Sicily, Salerno and Anzio during 1943 and 1944. Victories in Sicily and Italy were paralleled by Soviet successes in the East, with the winning of the battle for Stalingrad in February 1943 and the liberation of Sevastopol in May 1944. One month later,

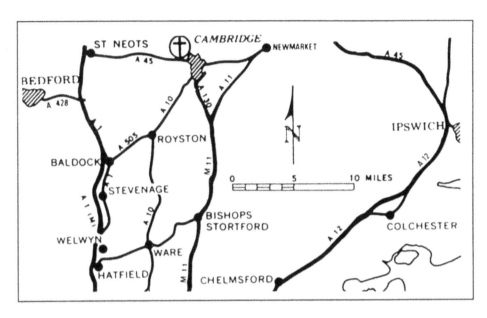

Allied forces entered Rome and the landings in Normandy commenced.

The third objective during the war against Germany was to conduct an intensive strategic bombardment of Germany in order to destroy its military, industrial and economic systems. Achievement of this objective depended on the use of air bases within the British Isles. As the airfields were constructed and expanded, the air war against Germany intensified the first American strategic bombing against a target in Europe took place in August 1942. By the end of the war, more than one-half million sorties against targets in western Europe were flown by British-based American aircraft.

The final objective was to invade the European continent and defeat the enemy on its historic battlefields. U.S. and British Commonwealth forces landed on the beaches of Normandy on 6 June 1944 in what was to be the greatest amphibious operation in the history of warfare. Supported by U.S. and British aircraft, the Allied ground forces fought their way across France and crossed into Germany in September of 1944.

With the Allied victory in Europe on 8 May 1945, the struggle against the enemy in the Pacific was intensified. Confronted by overwhelming military superiority, its major cities devastated and weakened by the defeat of the Axis in Europe, Japan surrendered on 2 September 1945.

Reflecting pool — Cambridge American Cemetery and Memorial.

CAMBRIDGE CEMETERY

Name & Rank	Unit	Gp	Pl-Row-Gr	Number	Date of Death	Cemetery
HENSLEE, RAY W. 1/ST	439BS	319	F-7-73	0-725975	12 NOV 42	CAMBRIDGE
SALTER, CARROLL F. T/SGT	439BS	319	D-6-47	19015586	12 NOV 42	CAMBRIDGE
ANDERSON, JOHN C. SGT	451BS	322	E-5-118	15075376	21 MAY 44	CAMBRIDGE
BOTSFORD, ROBERT C. 1/LT	HQ	322	E-0-61	0-567385	04 JUL 44	CAMBRIDGE
BRADFORD, JAMES E. S/SGT	451BS	322	F-6-38	1216625	21 MAY 44	CAMBRIDGE
BRENTINE, GEORGE F. 2/LT	452BS	322	B-4-37	0-816040	10 JUN 44	CAMBRIDGE
BRYANT, HENRY F. FLT/O	452BS	322	D-1-89	T-187570	29 MAY 43	CAMBRIDGE
CLARKE, WILLIAM D. JR. 1/LT	449BS	322	F-7-75	0-790795	14 AUG 43	CAMBRIDGE
ELEAZER, JAMES M. T/SGT	450BS	322	E-3-114	12079636	26 JUL 44	CAMBRIDGE
ELTZROTH, RALPH E. 1/LT	451BS	322	E-0-85	0-727324	21 JAN 44	CAMBRIDGE
GROSSKOPF, ROBERT C. 2/LT	451BS	322	C-5-47	0-813891	21 MAY 44	CAMBRIDGE
HART, FRANCIS V. S/SGT	451BS	322	A-5-13	32327026	25 MAY 44	CAMBRIDGE
HEIDELBERGER, LESLIE 2/LT	450BS	322	D-2-73	0-731065	25 APR 43	CAMBRIDGE
HENNING, CHESTER W. T/SGT	449BS	322	F-2-61	17052239	24 DEC 42	CAMBRIDGE
KNOY, GLENDALE CPL	451BS	322	D-1-55	35112724	12 JUN 43	CAMBRIDGE
LAREY, CAREY H. JR. 1/LT	450BS	322	E-6-30	0-791706	26 APR 43	CAMBRIDGE
McDONALD, JE J. S/SGT	451BS	322	C-1-78	18199430	21 MAY 44	CAMBRIDGE
McDONALD, ROBERT F. 1/LT	452BS	322	E-1-70	0-727241	29 MAY 43	CAMBRIDGE
McGUIRE, BERNARD J. 1/LT	452BS	322	D-5-29	0-663065	15 MAR 44	CAMBRIDGE
McWILLIAMS, EDWARD V. S/SGT	449BS	322	C-0-42	36129495	27 MAY 44	CAMBRIDGE
MOTHS, RUSSELL J. 2/LT	449BS	322	E-2-45	0-815204	16 AUG 44	CAMBRIDGE
PARKER, LAWRENCE E. S/SGT	449BS	322	F-3-134	37341420	19 AUG 44	CAMBRIDGE
REISS, JOHN W. 1/LT	449BS	322	F-3-78	0-664658	04 JUN 43	CAMBRIDGE
ROTES, PAUL N. T/SGT	451BS	322	F-5-101	35381922	21 JAN 44	CAMBRIDGE
SAPP, FLOYD K. SGT	451BS	322	E-5-108	12047726	21 MAY 44	CAMBRIDGE
SCHMIDT, DOUGALD R. 1/LT	449BS	322	A-1-1	0-664667	14 AUG 43	CAMBRIDGE
SCULL, HOWARD M. MAJ	HQ	322	C-2-30	0-381908	04 JUL 44	CAMBRIDGE
SHOOP, EARL W. 2/LT	449BS	322	D-5-79	0-796894	04 JUN 43	CAMBRIDGE
SPEIDEL, WILLIAM E, JR. SGT	450BS	322	E-5-90	32278575	26 APR 43	CAMBRIDGE
SWAIN, FLOYD E. 1/LT	450BS	322	F-3-41	0-744425	04 JUL 44	CAMBRIDGE
TAYLOR, BRUCE 2/LT	450BS	322	E-4-68	0-764829	12 AUG 44	CAMBRIDGE
WALKER, JOHNR. JR. 2/LT	450BS	322	E-6-58	0-814603	12 AUG 44	CAMBRIDGE
ANDERSON, ROBERT A. 2/LT	455BS	323	F-6-78	0-729949	03 JUN 43	CAMBRIDGE
ARCHER, WILLIAM F. S/SGT	453BS	323	C-3-26	14033874	12 SEPT 43	CAMBRIDGE
BOWEN, CHADWICK N. 1/LT	455BS	323	C-1-33	0-663007	09 AUG 43	CAMBRIDGE
CROSS, LEWIS M. M/SGT	455BS	323	D-7-99	14069227	03 JUN 43	CAMBRIDGE
FRANCIS, ROBERT J. S/SGT	455BS	323	E-0-88	31309090	13 JUN 45	CAMBRIDGE
KENYON, ALBERT W. S/SGT	455BS	323	B-7-6	31120793	09 AUG 43	CAMBRIDGE
LEATHAM, ARTHUS G. SGT	455BS	323	C-3-3	19073144	09 MAY 44	CAMBRIDGE
McKAIN, ROBERT C. SGT	454BS	323	F-6-132	39089857	19 MAY 44	CAMBRIDGE

Name & Rank	Unit	Gp	Pl-Row-Gr	Number	Date of Death	Cemetery
REDMOND, JOHN T/SGT	453BS	323	B-5-6	32218596	09 AUG 43	CAMBRIDGE
REMETTE, WILLIAM C. SGT	455BS	323	F-5-60	12040799	09 AUG 43	CAMBRIDGE
RUSH, LEO D. JR. 1/LT	456BS	323	F-3-127	0-678576	20 MAY 44	CAMBRIDGE
SATT, RALPH E. 2/LT	456BS	323	D-5-59	0-661873	13 JUNE 43	CAMBRIDGE
SCHUETTE, EILERT C. S/SGT	455BS	323	F-6-70	36243087	09 AUG 43	CAMBRIDGE
THOMPSON, DEWEY P. JR. T/SGT	454BS	323	F-5-22	14045442	29 FEB 44	CAMBRIDGE
BORDER, ALFRED R. S/SGT	494BS	344	C-4-40	17067585	08 MAR 44	CAMBRIDGE
BURGESS, JULIAN H. JR. 1/LT	497BS	344	C-4-24	0-684267	02 JUL 441	CAMBRIDGE
ECKERT, JOHN K. 1/LT	494BS	344	A-5-15	0-025692	08 MAR 44	CAMBRIDGE
MAYFIELD, CLEVELAND G. S/SGT	495BS	344	C-4-50	14141349	15 JUN 44	CAMBRIDGE
McMANNAMY, GEORGE D. S/SGT	494BS	344	F-2-77	06991524	08 MAR 44	CAMBRIDGE
O'CONNELL, RICHARD D. 2/LT	495BS	344	E-4-119	0-750092	25 AUG 44	CAMBRIDGE
VEALE, SIDNEY M. T/SGT	495BS	344	E-0-14	10600657	25 AUG 44	CAMBRIDGE
WHITLER, LEMAN E. JR. 1/LT	495BS	344	E-1-119	0-693085	25 AUG 44	CAMBRIDGE
WILLIAMS, EDWARD E. 1/LT	496BS	344	E-0-107	0-579664	30 AUG 44	CAMBRIDGE
WORRELL, THOMAS W. 2/LT	494BS	344	C-0-12	0-692598	08 MAR 44	CAMBRIDGE
AMBROSE, JAMES C. 2/LT	554BS	386	D-1-56	0-713989	16 SEPT 44	CAMBRIDGE
BRANDENBURG, JACK E. 1/LT	552BS	386	E-6-86	0-733140	08 APR 44	CAMBRIDGE
CARLSON, JOEL M. 1/LT	554BS	386	B-6-3	0-667939	08 FEB 44	CAMBRIDGE
COSTELLO, THOMAS C. 2/LT	553BS	386	F-4-78	0-567759	07 JUN 43	CAMBRIDGE
HUGHES, HARRY B. JR. 1/SGT	554BS	386	A-2-28	14081212	16 APR 44	CAMBRIDGE
LARSON, CAROL V. 1/LT	554BS	386	G-7-3	0-795777	10 AUG 44	CAMBRIDGE
McCLURE, HOMER R. 1/LT	555BS	386	D-6-73	0-668017	26 JAN 44	CAMBRIDGE
MELLEN, JAMES I. MAJ	HQ	386	D-6-79	0-422915	08 JUN 43	CAMBRIDGE
MORRIS, CHARLES M. S/SGT	555BS	386	F-6-58	15102501	26 JAN 44	CAMBRIDGE
PEARSON, JEFF L. 1/LT	555BS	386	F-6-100	0-667544	26 JAN 44	CAMBRIDGE
RODESCH, ROY K. CAPT		386	E-6-49	0-408924	27 AUG 44	CAMBRIDGE
RUSLANDER, SOLOMON L. 1/LT	553BS	386	D-4-96	01646153	13 SEPT 44	CAMBRIDGE
TANCK, DONALD D. 1/LT	554BS	386	F-4-64	0-670661	10 AUG 44	CAMBRIDGE
TURNER, EDWARD E. JR. MAJ	554BS	386	E-5-92	0-416585	16 SEPT 44	CAMBRIDGE
VOGIATZIS, GEORGE SGT	554BS	386	D-6-56	39038584	16 SEPT 44	CAMBRIDGE
BRANTLEY, JAMES H. 1/LT	556BS	387	F-7-11	0-663838	06-AUG 44	CAMBRIDGE
DEHANES, GEORGE PVT	559BS	387	F-7-15	32394053	14 JUL 44	CAMBRIDGE
GRIFFIN, DANIEL J. 2/LT	558BS	387	D-5-11	0-760053	18 JUL 44	CAMBRIDGE
LEVI, ALEXANDER W. 1/LT	557BS	387	E-6-25	0-732868	08 MAR 44	CAMBRIDGE
LOPEZ, MEDARDO T. S/SGT	559BS	387	E-2-81	38034397	09 SEPT 43	CAMBRIDGE
OGILVIE, PETER S/SGT	556BS	387	F-3-18	32409500	26 MAR 44	CAMBRIDGE
PATRICK, HENRY C. III 1/LT	559BS	387	A-2-32	0-793829	27 APR 44	CAMBRIDGE
SABIN, CLARENCE R. S/SGT	557BS	387	D-5-30	31124301	03 SEPT 43	CAMBRIDGE
TERRIO, CLEO C. 1/LT	556BS	387	C-6-41	0-732914	24 OCT 43	CAMBRIDGE
TIMERDING, WILLIAM C. 2/LT	558BS	387	E-0-70	0-810845	08 JUN 44	CAMBRIDGE

Name & Rank	Unit	Gp	Pl-Row-Gr	Number	Date of Death	Cemetery
BELL, WILLIAM J. SGT	573BS	391	G-7-160	19062484	28 MAY 44	CAMBRIDGE
CRIDER, JACOB E. III S/SGT	575BS	391	D-5-26	35482133	24 SEPT 44	CAMBRIDGE
DEMYANOVICH, EDWARD G. S/SGT	572BS	391	F-7-74	12145428	24 SEPT 44	CAMBRIDGE
KJOSNESS, GUSTAV D. 2/LT	572BS	391	F-2-83	0-671372	08 JUN 44	CAMBRIDGE
MYERS, JOHN M. CPL	572BS	391	E-3-115	160'14010	24 SEPT 44	CAMBRIDGE
NOLAND, HOWARD H. 2/LT	575BS	391	F-1-27	0-705412	24 SEPT 44	CAMBRIDGE
McCARTY, WILLIAM L. S/SGT	572BS	391	E-0-91	37196353	24 SEPT 44	CAMBRIDGE
TERRIAN, WARREN E. CPL	575BS	391	D-2-36	16089427	24 SEPT 44	CAMBRIDGE
BLADES, CHARLES E. S/SGT	584BS	394	E-1-94	06152184	18 JUL 44	CAMBRIDGE
KLINE, CLAUDE W. JR. 2/LT	587BS	394	E-0-58	0-686911	06 JUN 44	CAMBRIDGE
KYLE, GEORGE J. T/SGT	584BS	394	D-5-71	36348272	06 JUN 44	CAMBRIDGE
LUCE, ROBERT P. T/SGT	587BS	394	F-2-6	31100561	07 MAY 44	CAMBRIDGE
MONAGHAN, EDWARD H. S/SGT	587BS	394	F-5-67	32038614	06 JUN 44	CAMBRIDGE
RODGERS, WARREN D. 1/LT	587BS	394	B-5-37	0-688847	06 JUN 44	CAMBRIDGE
DOWNING, JAMES B. S/SGT	584BS	394	F-3-94	35576452	18 JUL 44	CAMBRIDGE
COOK, FREDERICK C. 2/LT	598BS	397	D-2-31	0-743568	17 JUN 44	CAMBRIDGE
CURRY, WILLIE S/SGT	599BS	397	F-7-113	38106817	09 JUL 44	CAMBRIDGE
EVANS, FRANK K. 1/LT	597BS	397	E-4-65	0796979	13 MAY 44	CAMBRIDGE
LAWLESS, MATTHEW S. PFC	598BS	397	E-5-19	32418744	29 MAY 44	CAMBRIDGE

Cambridge Cemetery.

EPINAL CEMETERY

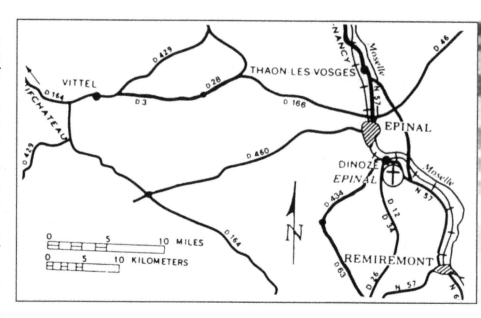

Epinal Cemetery is located 4 miles south of Epinal (Vosges), France, on the west bank of the Moselle River, 231 miles east of Paris.

The cemetery, 48 acres in extent, is situated on a plateau 100 feet above the river, in the foothills of the Vosges Mountains; it contains the graves of 5,255 of our military Dead, most of whom gave their lives in the campaigns across northeastern France to the Rhine and beyond into Germany.

The memorial, a rectangular structure with two large bas-relief panels, consists of a chapel, portico, and museum room with its mosaic operations map. On the walls of the Court of Honor, which surround the memorial, are inscribed the names of 424 of the Missing who gave their lives in the service of their Country and who rest in unknown graves.

Stretching northward is a wide tree-lined mall which separates the two large burial plots. At the northern end of the mall the circular flagpole plaza forms an overlook affording a view of a wide sweep of the Moselle Valley.

HISTORY

On 15 August 1944, just a little over two months after the landings in Normandy, Allied Forces launched an amphibious assault to free southern France. Air bombardment in preparation for the landings began in July and grew steadily in intensity. Preceded by Allied assault groups and U.S. airborne and glider troops, under cover of heavy naval and aerial bombardment, the 3rd, 36th and 45th Divisions of the U.S. VI Corps troops of the U.S. Seventh Army pursued the enemy, French units landed and moved westward toward Toulon and Marseilles. Within two weeks both ports had been liberated and U.S. forces had advanced northward up the Rhone Valley to seize Montelimar, cutting off large numbers of the retreating enemy.

In less than one month, U.S. troops from southern France had advanced 400 miles and made contact with those from Normandy on 11 September 1944 at Sombernon, west of Dijon. Ten days later, when these forces had joined in strength

near Epinal, a solid line was established extending to the Swiss frontier. Progress in the next three months was slow and fighting bitter, as opposition stiffened. Nevertheless, Allied Forces continued their advance to the Siegfried Line and westward to the Rhine River where our troops held the west bank except for an area between Strasbourg and Mulhouse known as the "Colmar Pocket."

The enemy launched his final major counteroffensive of the war on 16 December 1944. Officially designated the Ardennes-Alsace Campaign, it was popularly known at the "Battle of the Bulge." The U.S. Third Army to the north moved quickly to counter the threat. This required the 6th Army group in the south, consisting of the U.S. Seventh and the French First Armies, to extend its lines northward to cover a much longer front. Against this line, the enemy launched the second half of his planned counteroffensive on New Year's Eve by driving for the Saverne Gap in the Vosges Mountains and following with an attack across the Rhine and an offensive from the Colmar Pocket toward Strasbourg. After furious struggles in bitterly cold weather, all of these attacks were halted. Quickly, the American and French troops joined forces to eliminate the enemy army in the Colmar Pocket, their mission was successfully completed by 9 February 1945. The U.S. Seventh Army thereupon undertook a progressive assault against the Siegfried Line to the north, while the U.S. Third Army continued to assault the

The memorial at the Epinal Cemetery.

Line and the enemy's flanks and rear. Soon, the Siegfried Line was broken and the remaining enemy units cleared from the west bank of the Rhine.

The final offensive of the U.S. Seventh Army began in late March when it crossed the Rhine near Worms and seized Mannheim. Promptly, the French First Army crossed behind it and took Karlsruhe. Preceded by aircraft that constantly harassed and demoralized the enemy, Allied Forces swept throughout Germany. As the French captured Stuttgart and cut off escape into Switzerland, the U.S. Seventh Army fought through Nurnberg, took Munich, then drove through the Brenner Pass for its historic meeting with the U.S. Fifth Army on 4 May 1945 at Vipiteno, Italy.

EPINAL CEMETERY

Name & Rank	Unit	Gp	Pl-Row-Gr	Number	Date of Death	Cemetery
CASTON, VICTOR 2/LT	451BS	322	A-43-22	01996072	18 MAR 45	EPINAL
JOLLEY, JAMES J. JR. SGT	451BS	322	A-8-29	34808221	18 MAR 45	EPINAL
LAMB, THOMAS E. SGT	451BS	322	B-15-14	16160208	18 MAR 45	EPINAL
MIRELL, SEYMOUR S. 1/LT	451BS	322	B-27-60	0-735892	07 JAN 45	EPINAL
MOORE, JOSEPH E. JR. 1/LT	451BS	322	A-39-28	0-390039	22 JAN 45	EPINAL
MYERS, WESLEY M. 2/LT	451BS	322	A-31-59	0-765674	18 MAR 45	EPINAL
PRATT, JOE F. SGT	451BS	322	A-19-28	38513794	18 MAR 45	EPINAL
REGMUND, JOHN W. JR. 2/LT	451BS	322	B-14-14	02068121	18 MAR 45	EPINAL
RICE, ROY L. JR. 2/LT	451BS	322	B-7-64	0-824225	18 MAR 45	EPINAL
TEMPLETON, JOHN W. SGT	451BS	322	B-18-68	38344016	18 MAR 45	EPINAL
SPERON, STEVE J. S/SGT	454BS	323	A-47-17	36854103	26 OCT 44	EPINAL
CARLSON, NORMAN D. 1/LT	495BS	344	A-22-33	0-760155	27 DEC 44	EPINAL
COLLINS, ROBERT J. SGT	497BS	344	A-18-29	33232400	28 JAN 45	EPINAL
GERSTING, JOHN R. 2/LT	496BS	344	A-24-62	0-829613	28 MAR 45	EPINAL
GILMORE, ROBERT P. 1/LT	495BS	344	A-19-11	0-732458	28 MAY 44	EPINAL
HEDSTROM, WALTER H. 2/LT	496BS	344	A-31-55	0-719643	28 MAR 45	EPINAL
HERRIED, RICHARD S. CAPT	496BS	344	B-41-36	0-734344	14 HJAN 45	EPINAL
HILGER, LEWIS A. SGT	494BS	344	A-5-61	39619519	14 JAN 45	EPINAL
JOHNSTON, JAMES 1/LT	495BS	344	A-35-27	0-745816	28 MAY 44	EPINAL
LEWITTES, HUDAH H. 1/LT	497BS	344	A-16-64	0-700745	09 MAY 45	EPINAL
MADDOX, CLYDE S. T/SGT	495BS	344	B-12-68	18105661	28 MAY 44	EPINAL
MENDEZ, ESEQUIEL P. JR. S/SGT	494BS	344	A-25-28	18154888	14 JAN 45	EPINAL
MOFFETT, EUGENE D. 1/LT	495BS	344	B-3-64	0-669088	05 JUN 44	EPINAL
SWEENEY, OWEN B. JR. SGT	494BS	344	A-29-28	15324625	14 JAN 45	EPINAL
WILLIAMSON, ARTHUR M. 2/LT	496BS	344	A-32-62	20601790	28 MAR 45	EPINAL
ALLENBRAND, J. B. 2/LT	554BS	386	A-5-15	0-687522	10 FEB 45	EPINAL
BEADLE, FREDERICK J. SGT	553BS	386	1-21-33	39606520	29 DEC 44	EPINAL
BLEDSOE, ROBERT W. 2/LT	553BS	386	A-38-27	0-706116	29 DEC 44	EPINAL
BORRELL, RICHARD A. 1/LT	555BS	386	A-32-59	0-732462	13 OCT 44	EPINAL
ELLIS, JOHN T. JR. SGT	554BS	386	A-30-29	18131623	08 FEB 45	EPINAL
FLINN, WILLIAM II 1/LT	555BS	386	B-3-67	0-791684	05 OCT 44	EPINAL
GRAFF, DANIEL J. S/SGT	555BS	386	B-21-14	36018473	05 OCT 44	EPINAL
HICKS, WAYNE D. 2/LT	555BS	386	B-3-67	0-704292	05 OCT 44	EPINAL
JOHNSON, EVERETT G. 2/LT	555BS	386	B-3-67	0-815154	05 OCT 44	EPINAL
KELLY M. DONALD E. SGT	553BS	386	B-11-71	39700402	11 NOV 44	EPINAL
MILLER, URIAH W. 1/LT	554BS	386	A-14-64	0-688835	31 MAY 44	EPINAL
MORGAN, FRANK B. 1/LT	555BS	386	B-39-46	0-750431	20 DEC 44	EPINAL
REPETA, HENRY T/SGT	555BS	386	B-13-38	32453092	30 APR 44	EPINAL
TIGER, GLENN H. FLT/O	553BS	386	B-18-21	T-126259	11 NOV 44	EPINAL

Name & Rank	Unit	Gp	Pl-Row-Gr	Number	Date of Death	Cemetery
AU, DALE D. CPL	557BS	387	A-38-41	35423711	09 DEC 44	EPINAL
BOCH, JOSEPH F. SGT	559BS	387	A-13-53	35423782	09 DEC 44	EPINAL
CARBONNELL, JAMES A. SGT	558BS	387	A-34-33	3983998	16 FEB 45	EPINAL
FAULKNER, CHARLES J.I. 1/LT	557BS	387	B-36-40	9790-425	01 NOV 44	EPINAL
GLASS, WILLIAM G. S/SGT		387	B-42-36	33117765	22 JAN 45	EPINAL
HILL, ROBERT E. 2/LT	559BS	387	B-6-57	0-713440	30 NOV 44	EPINAL
HOLLEKIM, NORMAN J. 2/LT	559BS	387	A-6-23	0-697359	30 NOV 44	EPINAL
LEIPSE, ROBERT A. S/SGT	556BS	387	A-21-53	38529886	02 JAN 44	EPINAL
LONG, ROY V. SGT	559BS	387	B-30-37	18077309	30 NOV 44	EPINAL
McFADDEN, ELWIN J. 1/LT	558BS	387	B-36-50	0-742338	29 MAY 44	EPINAL
MORSE, ROBERT B. 2/LT	559BS	387	A-33-18	0-712205	30 NOV 44	EPINAL
PADGETT, JAMES W. JR. 2/LT	557BS	387	B-10-43	0-712213	24 NOV 44	EPINAL
REID, RAYMOND W. 2/LT	559BS	387	B-46-10	0-822090	16 APR 45	EPINAL
SHEHAN, ERNEST J. S/SGT	559BS	387	A-6-19	37192608	30 NOV 44	EPINAL
THOMPSON, GEORGE E. S/SGT	558BS	387	B-36-51	11023579	29 MAY 44	EPINAL
WATTERS, FRANKLIN L. CAPT	556BS	387	B-27-61	01686865	09 DEC 44	EPINAL
COE, WILLIAM J. T/SGT	573BS	391	A-23-29	13157796	16 JAN 45	EPINAL
EDWARDS, GEORGE A. JR. 1/LT	573BS	391	A-23-64	0-689950	16 JAN 45	EPINAL
GRIGSBY, WILLIAM T. CPL	572BS	391	A-16-33	38435144	15 OCT 44	EPINAL
KELLEY, HENRY J. JR 2/LT	572BS	391	A-12-46	0-749257	18 OCT 44	EPINAL
ZOBEL, CARL J. SGT	574BS	391	B-30-14	17114615	05 OCT 44	EPINAL
AYLWARD, RICHARD F. JR. S/SGT	585BS	394	B-5-13	31308752	02 DEC 44	EPINAL
CAMERON, LYNN T. S/SGT	587BS	394	A-26-64	17040903	14 JUN 44	EPINAL
CLEVENGER, RUSSELL H. 2/LT	587BS	394	B-6-53	0-719560	25 FEB 45	EPINAL
DELANO, WILLIAM E. SGT	587BS	394	A-32-52	42025208	25 FEB 45	EPINAL
DRAPER, HOWARD L. S/SGT	587BS	394	A-8-70	39238853	25 FEB 45	EPINAL
KEMNITZ, CHARLES A. 2/LT	584BS	394	B-32-54	0-758349	08 OCT 44	EPINAL
LESTER, HAROLD D. SGT	584BS	394	B-10-67	34635644	08 OCT 44	EPINAL
LYNCH, ANDREW B. JR. S/SGT	585BS	394	B-32-50	13028948	02 DEC 44	EPINAL
NEIS, ELMER J. T/SGT	587BS	394	A-18-27	37280296	14 JUN 44	EPINAL
OSS, BENJAMIN G. SGT	584BS	394	B-24-14	13001920	08 OCT 44	EPINAL
PICARD, JAMES L. S/SGT	587BS	394	B-6-68	31135417	14 JUN 44	EPINAL
ROBB, RICHARD K. 2/LT	584BS	394	B-20-71	0-712222	08 OCT 44	EPINAL
ROEPKE, FRANK W. JR. 2/LT	584BS	394	B-40-14	0-699632	08 OCT 44	EPINAL
ROSE, PAUL E. SGT	584BS	394	B-7-67	1911-652	08 OCT 44	EPINAL
SKISCIM, JOHN A. 1/LT	587BS	394	B-5-68	0-712319	23 FEB 45	EPINAL
SMITH, WESLEY V. JR. 2/LT	584BS	394	B-22-14	0-822836	08 OCT 44	EPINAL
WADDELL, CHARLES F. 2/LT	587BS	394	A-27-64	0-760141	14 JUN 44	EPINAL
WILLIAMS, MANETHO JR. S/SGT	587BS	394	A-14-43	33150139	25 FEB 45	EPINAL
WILSON, DONALD E. S/SGT	585BS	394	B-31-22	15016611	09 AUG 44	EPINAL
BOOTH, ROBERT L. 1/LT	598BS	397	B-31-31	0-766190	11 MAR 45	EPINAL

Name & Rank	Unit	Gp	Pl-Row-Gr	Number	Date of Death	Cemetery
BRODLEY, FRANCIS W. SGT	597BS	397	A-5-43	11058151	26 FEB 45	EPINAL
CLARK, IRVING F. 1/LT	598BS	397	A-11-71	0-668049	11 MAR 45	EPINAL
FRANK, ELMER J. 1/LT	597BS	397	B-26-43	0-815873	19 APR 45	EPINAL
HURST, DAREN H. S/SGT	598BS	397	B-38-31	18132770	11 MAR 45	EPINAL
KEMP, BILLY D. FLT/O	597BS	397	A-12-42	T-129084	14 FEB 45	EPINAL
LEUPOLD, DONALD H. S/SGT	597BS	397	B-28-61	16130869	14 FEB 45	EPINAL
LINDQUIST, EDWARD M. 2/LT	597BS	397	A-23-28	0-746663	24 JUN 44	EPINAL
LOBECK, DAVID L. 1/LT	598BS	397	B-5-53	0-721137	08 AUG 45	EPINAL
NEILL, SAMUEL C. 2/LT	597BS	397	B-19-15	0-687700	24 JUN 44	EPINAL
POTSCHNER, JOHN T. 2/LT	597BS	397	A-15-43	0-719733	26 FEB 45	EPINAL
RICHARDS, JAMES A. PFC	596BS	397	A-28-63	39167111	09 SEPT 45	EPINAL
SMITH, FRANCIS L. JR. FLT/O	598BS	397	A-10-53	T-005626	22 JAN 45	EPINAL
VORHEES, HAROLD G. S/SGT	597BS	397	A-44-25	13011177	24 JUN 44	EPINAL
WISE, COLIN R. T/SGT	598BS	397	A-8-65	12038193	11 MAR 45	EPINAL

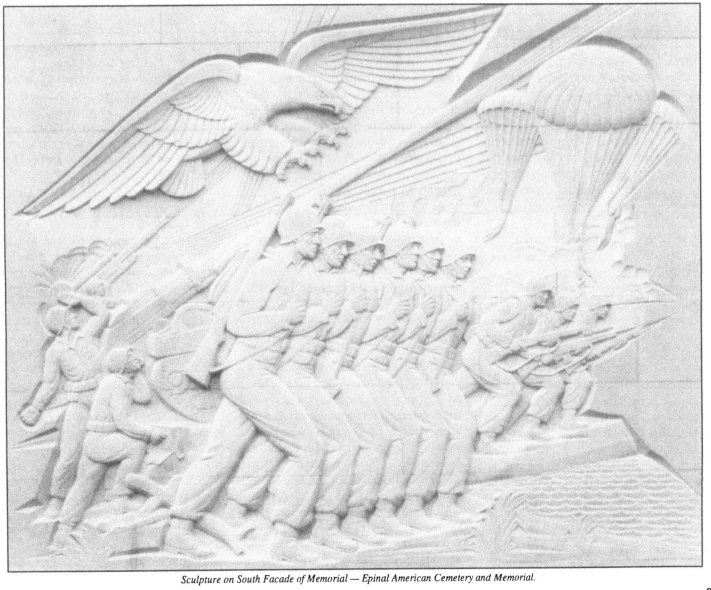

Sculpture on South Facade of Memorial — Epinal American Cemetery and Memorial.

HENRI-CHAPELLE CEMETERY

Henri-Chapelle Cemetery lies 2 miles northwest of the village of Henri-Chapelle which is on the main highway from Liege, Belgium (18 miles) to Aachen, Germany (10 miles).

At this cemetery, covering 57 acres, rest 7,989 of our military Dead, most of whom gave their lives during the advance of the U.S. Armed Forces into Germany. Their headstones are arranged in graceful arcs sweeping across a broad green lawn which slopes gently downhill.

A highway passes through the reservation. West of the highway an overlook affords an excellent view of the rolling Belgian countryside, once a battlefield.

To the east is the long colonnade which, with the chapel and museum room, forms the memorial overlooking the burial area. The chapel is simple but richly ornamented. In the museum are two maps of military operation, carved in black granite, with inscriptions recalling the achievements of our Forces.

On the rectangular piers of the colonnade are inscribed the names of 450 of the Missing who gave their lives in the service of their County. The seals of the states and territories are also carved on these piers.

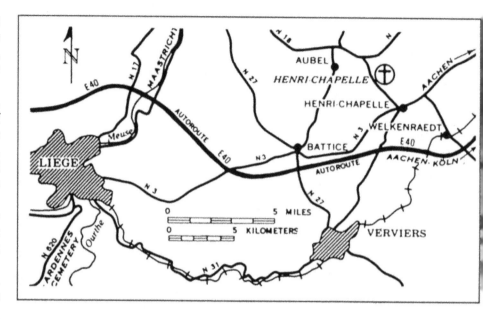

HISTORY

The Siegfried Line formed the core of resistance at the center of the enemy defenses. To the south in front of the U.S. Third and Seventh Armies, and the French First Army which extended Allied lines to the Swiss border, resistance was organized around heavily fortified cities forming strong points in front of the Siegfried Line. In the north, the defenders utilized to advantage against the British and Canadians the barriers formed by the extensive canal and river systems. On 17 September, a valiant combined airborne-ground assault in the Netherlands intended to outflank the north end of the enemy line, achieved only partial success as it failed to seize crossings of the lower Rhine.

For the next three months, intensive fighting produced only limited gains against fierce opposition. During this period, the principal Allied offensive effort was concentrated in the center of the enemy line where some of the most bitter fighting of the war occurred in the battle to capture the city of Aachen, the first large German city to be captured by the Allies, and penetrate the Siegfried Line. Finally, encircled in mid-October after savage house-to-house fighting, Aachen fell on 21 October. Meanwhile, the U.S. Ninth Army organized at Brest in Brittany, moved into the lines on the left flank of the U.S. First Army. To the south, the U.S. Third and Seventh Armies continued to advance slowly, as the U.S. Seventh Army forced the enemy back into the Vosges Mountains.

On 4 November, the U.S. First Army began the difficult struggle through the dense woods of the Hurtgen Forest. Shortly thereafter, the U.S. Ninth Army was shifted to the U.S. First Army's left flank. Then, on 16 November preceded by a massive air bombardment, the two armies attacked together opening a wide gap in the Siegfried Line. By 1 December, the Roer River line was reached. On the right, the city of Metz was captured by the U.S. Third Army on 22 November, although the last fort defending that city did not surrender until 13 December. The greatest territorial gains, however, came in the south where the U.S. Seventh Army penetrated the Vosges Mountains to liberate the city of Strasbourg on 23 November as French troops on the extreme right flank liberated Mulhouse.

The Schelde estuary was finally cleared of the enemy by the Canadian First Army and the great port city of Antwerp became available on 28 November to supply the Allied armies.

Suddenly on 16 December 1944, the Allied advance was interrupted when the enemy launched in the Ardennes its final major counteroffensive of the war, with a second major assault on New Year's Eve in Alsace to the south. After furious fighting in bitterly cold weather these last enemy onslaughts were halted and the lost ground regained. The Allies then developed their plan for final victory.

The first step of the plan was to clear all enemy troops from west of the Rhine; the subsequent step was to invade Germany itself. During February and March, with the aid and assistance of fighters and medium bombers, the first step was successfully completed and heavy losses were inflicted on the enemy. Because of those losses, the subsequent crossing of the Rhine did not meet with the violent opposition that had been anticipated. Working together, Allied ground and air forces swept victoriously across Germany, bringing the war in Europe to a conclusion on 8 May 1945.

Henri-Chapelle Cemetery with the memorial overlooking the burial area.

The Guardian Angel — Henri-Chapelle American Cemetery and Memorial.

HENRI-CHAPELLE CEMETERY

Name & Rank	Unit	Gp	Pl-Row-Gr	Number	Date of Death	Cemetery
GIBSON, ROY J. 2/LT	449BS	322	H-9-22	0-715189	12 DEC 44	HENRI - CHAPELLE
HARRIS, GEORGE P. 1/LT	449BS	322	G-5-2	0-715965	12 DEC 44	HENRI - CHAPELLE
SMITH, VIRGIL T/SGT	453BS	323	E-13-37	16049634	14 JAN 45	HENRI - CHAPELLE
ALLYN, WEBSTER S. CAPT	494BS	344	H-3-64	0-727146	19 NOV 44	HENRI - CHAPELLE
BLUE, VERNON 1/LT	553BS	386	G-13-29	0-818561	28 NOV 44	HENRI - CHAPELLE
CUBBA, LOUIS J. S/SGT	554BS	386	H-8-59	36526010	23 SPET 44	HENRI - CHAPELLE
BOETTCHER, JOHN H. SGT	572BS	391	F-5-49	39214440	24 FEB 45	HENRI - CHAPELLE
RAIMONDE, PAUL S/SGT	574BS	391	H-12-71	32871884	23 DEC 44	HENRI - CHAPELLE
SWANSON, WILLIAM C. T/SGT	574BS	391	G-3-40	32422413	23 DEC 44	HENRI - CHAPELLE
ARZOUIAN, JACOB CPL	586BS	394	G-5-15	12208834	18 DEC 44	HENRI - CHAPELLE
BRASHEAR, LAWRENCE C. CPL	586BS	394	E-14-57	17132497	18 DEC 44	HENRI - CHAPELLE
BUNTING, HORACE O. CPL	586BS	394	G-4-23	36676498	18 DEC 44	HENRI - CHAPELLE
CHERESCAVICH, VINCENT CPL	586BS	394	G-4-24	42004669	18 DEC 44	HENRI - CHAPELLE
CLEARWATER, GEORGE W. 2/LT	586BS	394	G-15-30	0-721645	18 DEC 44	HENRI - CHAPELLE
DERITIS, CHARLES J. CAPT	586BS	394	D-10-21	0-793080	18 NOV 44	HENRI - CHAPELLE
DI LUZIO, ALBERT J. T/SGT	586BS	394	E-9-70	13086118	18 NOV 44	HENRI - CHAPELLE
KELLEY, THOMAS M. 2/LT	586BS	394	G-9-63	0-762174	02 DEC 44	HENRI - CHAPELLE
THOMPSON, EDWARD A. 2/LT	586BS	394	H-9-25	0-821377	18 DEC 44	HENRI - CHAPELLE
WITTE, KENNETH W. SGT	586BS	394	G-9-3	33718370	02 DEC 44	HENRI - CHAPELLE
WOJS, JOHN L. SGT	586BS	394	G-9-2	36316583	02 DEC 44	HENRI - CHAPELLE
WOLFF, GEORGE F. S/SGT	585BS	394	G-5-1	16089923	10 DEC 44	HENRI - CHAPELLE
BARTHO, FRANK A. SGT		397	H-10-16	36515344	10 NOV 44	HENRI - CHAPELLE
BURNS, WILLIAM J. PVT	598BS	397	E-3-76	31170883	10 JAN 45	HENRI - CHAPELLE
CULLEN, EDWARD CPL	598BS	397	E-1-26	31299800	10 JAN 45	HENRI - CHAPELLE

LORRAINE CEMETERY

Lorraine Cemetery is situated 1/4 mile north of the town of St. Avold (Moselle), France. St. Avold is 28 miles east of Metz, 17 miles southwest of Saarbrucken, and 220 miles northeast of Paris.

The cemetery, which covers 113 1/2 acres, contains the largest number of graves of our military Dead of World War II in Europe, a total of 10,489. Most of these lost their lives while fighting in this region. Their headstones are arranged in nine plots in a generally elliptical design extending over the beautiful rolling terrain of eastern Lorraine and culminating in a prominent overlook feature.

The memorial, which stands on a plateau to the west of the burial area, contains ceramic operations maps with narratives and service flags. High on its exterior front wall is the large figure of St. Nabor, the martyred Roman soldier, who overlooks the silent host. On each side of the memorial, and parallel to its front, stretch the walls of the Missing on which are inscribed the names of 444 Americans who gave their lives in the service of their Country but who remains were not recovered or identified. The entire area is enframed in woodland.

HISTORY

The U.S. Third Army resumed its pursuit of the enemy across France early in September 1944, after a brief halt because of a shortage of fuel. Except at Metz, where extremely heavy fortifications and resistance were encountered, the U.S. Third Army advanced rapidly and crossed the Moselle River. By late September, Nancy was liberated and a juncture with the U.S. Seventh Army, which was advancing northward from the beaches of southern France, was made near Epinal. Upon the joining of these two Armies, a solid Allied front was established extending to the Swiss border.

Throughout October, the two Armies pushed aggressively eastward against increasingly strong resistance. The U.S. Third Army drove toward the Saar River and the U.S. Seventh Army into the Vosges Mountains, as the enemy fortress at Metz continued to resist. On 8 November 1944, the U.S.

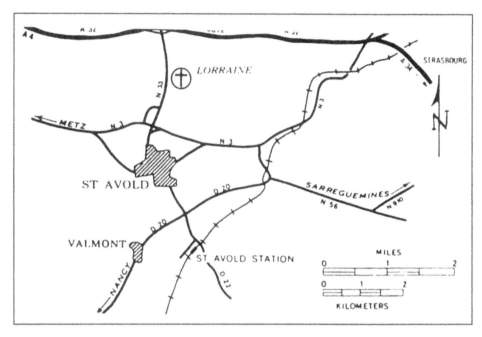

Third Army launched a major offensive toward the Saar River. During this offensive, the main fortress at Metz was encircled and it capitulated on 22 November. Its outer forts, however, did not surrender until 13 December. By passing this resistance, the U.S. Third Army continued to advance, capturing Saarguemines on 6 December 1944. By mid-December, several bridgeheads had been established across the Saar River and the U.S. Third Army had begun preparations for breaching the Siegfried Line. Meanwhile on 11 November, the U.S. Seventh Army to the south launched an attack eastward capturing Saarebourg on 20 November 1944. Moving rapidly, it outflanked, then penetrated the vital Saverne Gap in the Vosges Mountains. Sending the French 2d Armored Division to liberate Strasbourg on the Rhine River, the U.S. Seventh Army turned northward advancing along the west bank of the Rhine against the defenses of the Siegfried Line, simultaneously aiding the U.S. Third Army's operations to the north.

Throughout these operations, the U.S. Ninth Air Force and the U.S. First Tactical Air Force rendered vital air support to the U.S. Third Army's operations to the north.

Throughout these operations, the U.S. Ninth Air Force and the U.S. First Tactical

Air Force rendered vital air support to the U.S. Third and Seventh Armies, respectively, despite severe rainstorms and cold weather.

The progress of the two U.S. armies was halted temporarily by the enemy's final major counteroffensive of the war, which began in the Ardennes Forest on 16 December 1944. Officially designated the Ardennes-Alsace Campaign, it became known as the "Battle of the Bulge." The U.S. Third Army moved quickly northward to counter this threat, as the U.S. Seventh Army and the French First Army to its south extended their lines northward to cover more front. The second phase of the enemy's final counteroffensive was launched on New Year's Eve against the U.S. Seventh Army and the French First Army. The assault began as a drive for the Saverne Gap followed by an attack across the Rhine toward Strasbourg. After furious fighting on all fronts in bitterly cold weather, the last major enemy offensive was halted and the U. S. Third and Seventh Armies resumed their assault on the Siegfried Line. The line was soon broken and all enemy units were cleared from the west bank of the Rhine. In March 1945, the two U.S. armies crossed the Rhine River and began their drive into Germany.

Left: Altar in the Chapel with sculptured figures of youth and religious and military heroes who throughout history have taken part in the struggle for freedom — Lorraine American Cemetery and Memorial. Bottom: Lorraine Cemetery with the memorial in the background.

LORRAINE CEMETERY

Name & Rank	Unit	Gp	Pl-Row-Gr	Number	Date of Death	Cemetery
FOSS, BENSON N. SGT	449BS	322	K-31-15	19055307	22 MAR 45	LORRAINE
GAUDETTE, GEORGE J. JR. 1/LT	450BS	322	D-19-38	0-753340	05 AUG 45	LORRAINE
HALL, ROBERT R. CAPT	452BS	322	K-10-19	0-42761	09 NOV 44	LORRAINE
JACKSON, DOUGLAS D. SGT	451BS	322	J-23-23	18098916	09 NOV 44	LORRAINE
McLAUGHLIN, GEORGE D. 2/LT	451BS	322	J-35-36	0-715929	09 NOV 44	LORRAINE
RYAN, ROBERT W. SGT	452BS	322	A-29-48	15084322	09 NOV 44	LORRAINE
SACHS, PHILIP 2/LT	451BS	322	B-32-12	0-722679	09 NOV 44	LORRAINE
SZEWCZAK, HAROLD SGT	449BS	322	K-31-37	33831221	22 MAR 45	LORRAINE
BLAIN, LUCIEN F. SGT	453BS	323	C-16-66	11041447	05 JUNE 45	LORRAINE
CHOATE, FLOURNEY L. JR. 1/LT	495BS	344	G-6-11	02058705	10 SEPT 45	LORRAINE
FISHER, GEORGE L. 2/LT	494BS	344	D-46-18	02066323	01 NOV 45	LORRAINE
FREDERICK, ALBERT C. FLT/O	495BS	344	D-19-19	T-134196	10 SEPT 45	LORRAINE
HICKS, PHILLIPS E. SGT	496BS	344	A-22-51	17136773	24 MAR 45	LORRAINE
LAZOWSKI, PHILIP L. S/SGT	495BS	344	J-18-24	31304626	01 NOV 45	LORRAINE
LUNO, LEROY L. FLT/O	495BS	344	K-33-26	T-133780	10 SEPT 45	LORRAINE
ROGERS, PUGH G. M/SGT	495BS	344	G-8-26	14073395	10 SEPT 45	LORRAINE
SMITH C. R ROY SGT	496BS	344	E-14-25	18232534	24 MAR 45	LORRAINE
STURN, ROBERT A. FLT/O	496BS	344	A-23-22	T-134267	24 MAR 45	LORRAINE
WHITE, FREDERICK F. FLT/O	496BS	344	A-22-23	T-133662	24 MAR 45	LORRAINE
WOODDY, ROY L. JR. CPL	495BS	344	E-19-37	39716958	01 NOV 45	LORRAINE
OWEN, ROBERT J. JR. CAPT	555BS	386	A-15-52	0-667542	18 NOV 44	LORRAINE
PARDRIDGE, JOHN R. 1/LT	554BS	386	C-17-27	0-676597	31 MAR 45	LORRAINE
PRICE, THOMAS U. S/SGT	555BS	386	K-40-24	12199029	18 NOV 44	LORRAINE
BANGERT, FRED F. 2/LT	556BS	387	C-8-82	0-779049	12 APR 45	LORRAINE
BATES, RODMAN W. 1/LT	556BS	387	C-16-93	01285695	12 APR 45	LORRAINE
ENGLISH, RAYMOND C. SGT	556BS	387	A-22-47	36853022	18 MAR 45	LORRAINE
HOMER, ARTHUR JR. S/SGT	556BS	387	E-30-29	31211102	12 APR 45	LORRAINE
HULSEY, ERSKINE L. 1/LT	558BS	387	K-27-4	0-689237	06 DEC 44	LORRAINE
KALAS, GERALD G. SGT	556BS	387	K-16-11	36652085	09 APR 45	LORRAINE
MALDONADO, CARLOS M. SGT	558BS	387	E-13-18	32810763	12 OCT 44	LORRAINE
PALLONE, JOSEPH M. 2/LT	556BS	387	B-28-6	0-831781	18 MAR 45	LORRAINE
PARKER, EDWARD J, JR. S/SGT	556BS	387	C-9-89	13156344	18 MAR 45	LORRAINE
SCALZO, JOHN J. SGT	556BS	387	K-22-22	33423161	09 APR 45	LORRAINE
ABRAHAM, CLAYTON S. 1/LT	573BS	391	B-20-25	0-751078	23 DEC 44	LORRAINE
BRANDON, DONALD K. LT/COL	HQ	391	E-14-31	0-388874	23 DEC 44	LORRAINE
BUCKLEY, DANIEL J. S/SGT	574BS	391	D-6-31	12037426	23 DEC 44	LORRAINE

Name & Rank	Unit	Gp	Pl-Row-Gr	Number	Date of Death	Cemetery
BUCKLEY, ROBERT D. S/SGT	574BS	391	K-14-6	17151527	23 DEC 44	LORRAINE
COWART, MILTON E. S/SGT	575BS	391	C-28-27	18190494	23 DEC 44	LORRAINE
COX, WILBUR G CAPT	573BS	391	E-10-23	0-791676	23 DEC 44	LORRAINE
DEAN, MILTON L. JR. S/SGT	574BS	391	E-31-23	38389353	23 DEC 44	LORRAINE
HAWKINSON, WILLIAM D. 2/LT	575BS	391	G-9-7	0-704289	23 DEC 44	LORRAINE
HULTON, JOHN V. 2/LT	575BS	391	D-12-31	0-822009	23 DEC 44	LORRAINE
KLOEPFER, WILLIAM A. 1/LT	575BS	391	D-13-31	0-681120	23 DEC 44	LORRAINE
LEMON, FLOYD R. T/SGT	573BS	391	B-19-25	15017620	23 DEC 44	LORRAINE
MICKELSON, CLARENCE E. 1/LT	574BS	391	E-20-31	0-705037	23 DEC 44	LORRAINE
NETECKE, THOMAS M. S/SGT	574BS	391	A-16-60	16168989	23 DEC 44	LORRAINE
WEISSKER, WILLIAM L. S/SGT	575BS	391	C-14-27	14070304	23 DEC 44	LORRAINE
WILSON, WOODROW S/SGT	573BS	391	K-15-19	13106559	23 DEC 44	LORRAINE
BELL, T. J. SGT	584BS	394	K-13-16	38477909	23 DEC 44	LORRAINE
BROWN, HAROLD T/SGT	584BS	394	K-44-32	13124369	19 FEB 45	LORRAINE
HARTER, MARTIN L CAPT	584BS	394	A-22-35	0-026288	19 FEB 45	LORRAINE
LUBECK, LEONARD CPL		394	A-16-35	31432960	04 DEC 45	LORRAINE
MENDELSOHN, JEROME H. SGT	584BS	394	J-50-19	32538446	23 DEC 44	LORRAINE
RIEGNER, FRED E. JR 2/LT	584BS	394	J-50-18	0-820060	23 DEC 44	LORRAINE
STRUBE, JSOEPH JR. S/SGT	584BS	394	E-7-31	32528327	02 MAR 45	LORRAINE
WHITE, WILLIAM M. 2/LT	587BS	394	K-31-28	0-693441	14 JUN 44	LORRAINE
ANDERSON, BENJAMIN J. S/SGT	597BS	397	A-14-51	37088900	13 MAR 45	LORRAINE
BAUER, UBALD L. 1/LT	598BS	397	K-34-34	0-738071	13 MAR 45	LORRAINE
GUILMETTE, NORMAN A. FLT/O	597BS	397	D-30-26	T-133683	28 MAR 45	LORRAINE
JACKSON, GERALD DEVER S/SGT	599BS	397	K-35-29	16113566	23 DEC 44	LORRAINE
MATHIS, BRYAN JR. 1/LT	598BS	397	A-13-60	0-781622	13 MAR 45	LORRAINE
NICKOLLS, JOHN R. S/SGT	598BS	397	G-13-25	37674259	13 MAR 45	LORRAINE
POTTS. RICHARD F. 1/LT	599BS	397	K-33-28	0-662979	25 DEC 44	LORRAINE
SCANDIFF, RALPH T. SGT	597BS	397	E-40-16	16137483	28 MAR 45	LORRAINE
SHEPARD, RONALD F. 1/LT	598BS	397	B-27-26	0-816165	18 MAR 45	LORRAINE
WRIGHT, JOSEPH L. 1/LT	598BS	397	E-44-36	0-708988	13 MAR 45	LORRAINE

LUXEMBOURG CEMETERY

Luxembourg Cemetery lies just within the limits of Luxembourg City, 3 miles east of the center of the capital, 248 miles northeast of Paris.

The cemetery, 50 1/2 acres in extent, is situated in a beautiful wooded area. Not far from the entrance stands the white stone chapel, set on a wide circular platform surrounded by woods. It is embellished with sculpture in bronze and stone, a stained-glass window with American unit insignia and a mosaic ceiling. Flanking the chapel at a lower level are two large stone pylons upon which are maps made of various inlaid granites, with inscriptions recalling the achievement of the American Armed Forces in this region. On the same pylons are inscribed the names of 371 of the Missing who gave their lives in the service of their Country, but whose remains were never recovered or identified.

Sloping gently downhill from the memorial is the burial area containing 5,076 of our military Dead, many of whom gave their lives in the "Battle of the Bulge" and in the advance to the Rhine. Their headstones follow along graceful curves, trees, fountains and flower beds contribute to the dignity of the ensemble.

Among those interred at the cemetery are the remains of General George S. Patton, Commander of the U.S. Third Army.

HISTORY

On 16 December 1944, the enemy in Europe launched his last major counteroffensive of the war. For the location of his attack, he chose the Ardennes Forest where his first breakthrough had achieved such tremendous success in 1940. Prepared in the greatest of secrecy, the plan called for three armies abreast to attack on a narrow front toward the west with Antwerp as its objective. The attack was timed to coincide with inclement weather in order to limit the use of Allied air power. The assault began at 0530 hours under the cover of fog and rain

and initially was quite successful as the enemy broke through on a 45-mile front. American soldiers resisted valiantly, however, and with heroic effort were able to hold the shoulders of the salient, blocking all attempts to expand the width of the penetration.

Available U.S. reserves were rushed to the scene of battle. At St. Vith, a furious struggle prevented the enemy's use of its vital road junction for a crucial period. In Bastogne, at the other vital road junction, American defenders clung tenaciously to their positions even though they had been surrounded for five days. Despite a penetration by some units of over 60 miles, the enemy was unable to exploit the breakthrough.

On 22 December 1944, the U.S. Third Army launched a strong counterattack against the southern flank of the penetration. The next day the skies cleared sufficiently to permit the U.S. Eighth and Ninth Air Forces to join the battle and to drop supplies to the defenders at Bastogne. Driving relentlessly forward despite strong opposition and bitterly cold weather, the U.S. Third Army broke through the enemy cordon around Bastogne

on 26 December. The U.S. First Army counterattacked from the north on 3 January 1945 and ten days later met with the U.S. Third Army at Houffalize. By 25 January, the enemy salient no longer existed.

In February, the U.S. Third Army drove the enemy from Luxembourg and breached the Siegfried Line. After capturing Trier, it continued its advance, seizing bridgeheads across the Kyll River and launching an attack to reach the Rhine. The U.S. Third Army units north of the Moselle River advanced first, covered by fighters and bombers of the U.S. Ninth Air Force. In just five days, they swept forward to join the U.S. First Army. By 10 March, all enemy units were cleared from the west bank of the Rhine north of its junction with the Moselle at Koblenz.

On 13 March, U.S. Third Army troops north of the Moselle River turned to the southeast to attack in coordination with the U.S. Third Army troops advancing south of the river. By 21 March, the entire west bank of the Rhine had been cleared in the U.S. Third Army sector. The next night, in a surprise assault, the U.S. Third Army crossed the Rhine at Oppenheim, a prelude to the final offensive of the war.

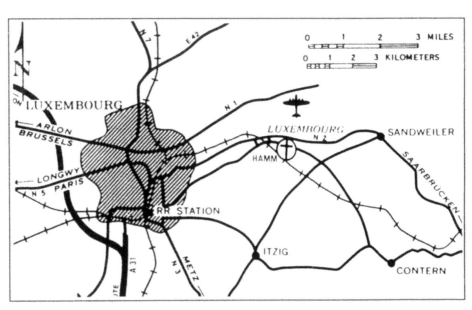

Left: Angel of Peace sculpture on the front of the Memorial — Luxembourg American Cemetery and Memorial. Bottom: Luxembourg American Cemetery.

LUXEMBOURG CEMETERY

Name & Rank	Unit	Gp	Pl-Row-Gr	Number	Date of Death	Cemetery
HANDS, ALBERT J. S/SGT	451BS	322	H-10-22	32179521	01 JAN 45	LUXEMBOURG
HARRIMAN, A. W. S/SGT	451BS	322	H-10-8	18168148	01 JAN 45	LUXEMBOURG
McCORMICK, VANCE I. 2/LT	451BS	322	D-5-17	0-765705	01 JAN 45	LUXEMBOURG
WEIR, ROBERT L. 2/LT	451BS	322	H-10-21	0-780774	01 JAN 45	LUXEMBOURG
HASSETT, JOHN T. FLT/O	496BS	344	E-6-16	T-127178	04 APR 45	LUXEMBOURG
LA FOUNTAINE, FREDERICK 2/LT	495BS	344	B-5-5	0-714713	14 FEB 45	LUXEMBOURG
DAWSON, HENRY A. SGT	553BS	386	A-4-9	36583366	15 DEC 44	LUXEMBOURG
HAAR, HAROLD E. SGT	553BS	386	B-1-13	12040500	15 DEC 44	LUXEMBOURG
JENKINS, THOMAS W. 2/LT	553BS	386	H-14-24	0-886067	09 MAR 45	LUXEMBOURG
NEWMAN, JEFF D. CAPT	559BS	387	B-3-51	0-663303	23 DEC 44	LUXEMBOURG
PORTER, FRANK C. S/SGT	559BS	387	E-14-30	19125019	23 DEC 44	LUXEMBOURG
STITH, GEORGE N. 1/LT	557BS	387	B-8-50	0-697177	23 DEC 44	LUXEMBOURG
WALDRON, AUBREY E. JR. CPL	559BS	387	C-9-5	36566581	23 DEC 44	LUXEMBOURG
BISHOP, GEORGE M. 2/LT	574BS	391	A-9-4	0-715127	23 DEC 44	LUXEMBOURG
BLAIR, JOSEPH M. 2/LT	574BS	391	D-3-17	0-558793	23 DEC 44	LUXEMBOURG
CASTLE, MARK W. 2/LT	575BS	391	C-6-6	0-927500	23 DEC 44	LUXEMBOURG
ESTREM, PAUL J. 2/LT	574BS	391	B-3-43	0-765475	23 DEC 44	LUXEMBOURG
HASQUIN, FELICIEN JR. CPL	574BS	391	G-2-17	36485250	23 DEC 44	LUXEMBOURG
HUSKEYM WILLIAM M, 1/LT	574BS	391	B-5-14	0-664608	24 FEB 45	LUXEMBOURG
KAYE, FREDERICK T. 2/LT	574BS	391	G-9-9	0-713468	23 DEC 44	LUXEMBOURG
PEREIRA, JOSEPH F. JR. FLT/O	574BS	391	F-4-16	T-136579	08 JUN 45	LUXEMBOURG
REISER, TED A. 2/LT	574BS	391	D-8-17	02068247	24 FEB 45	LUXEMBOURG
WILKINSON, PATRICK H. 1/LT	575BS	391	H-16-37	0-666110	23 DEC 44	LUXEMBOURG
BRUGMAN, ROBERT L 1/LT	584BS	394	A-5-19	0-744178	19 FEB 45	LUXEMBOURG
COSTA, LOUIS J. SGT	586BS	394	A-3-21	32432463	23 JAN 45	LUXEMBOURG
GENDERS, WILLIAM E 2/LT	586BS	394	B-1-8	0-783255	23 JAN 45	LUXEMBOURG
LINDEN, HERBERT M. M/SGT	586BS	394	H-9-12	18046911	04 APR 45	LUXEMBOURG
PROFFITT, DOYLE B. 2/LT	584BS	394	C-2-9	02064437	02 MAR 45	LUXEMBOURG
VOLLONO, VINCENT E. 2/LT	586BS	394	A-4-16	0-833846	23 JAN 45	LUXEMBOURG
BORDEN, ELMER R. 1/LT	599BS	397	A-5-9	0-746685	23 DEC 44	LUXEMBOURG
BOWER, WILLIAM E. T/SGT	599BS	397	E-15-34	15377068	23 DEC 44	LUXEMBOURG
DRULINER, DONALD R. 2/LT	599BS	397	B-9-3	0-719584	25 DEC 44	LUXEMBOURG
HEJNAR, JOSEPH W. SGT	598BS	397	B-7-34	33599667	23 DEC 44	LUXEMBOURG
HOOTS, JAMES A. SGT	598BS	397	C-1-16	36476466	23 DEC 44	LUXEMBOURG
KINNEY, ROBERT J. 1/LT	599BS	397	A-5-8	0-685642	23 DEC 44	LUXEMBOURG
McCARTHY, ROBERT E. 1/LT	599BS	397	E-4-38	0-684365	23 DEC 44	LUXEMBOURG

Name & Rank	Unit	Gp	Pl-Row-Gr	Number	Date of Death	Cemetery
PERKINS, HAROLD W. T/SGT	598BS	397	D-12-21	3755298	23 DEC 44	LUXEMBOURG
PORTANOVA, VITO S/SGT	599BS	397	B-1-28	12173751	23 DEC 44	LUXEMBOURG
PTASZKIEWICZ, HAROLD 2/LT	599BS	397	H-7-62	02061257	23 DEC 44	LUXEMBOURG
REED, KEITH C. 2/LT	597BS	397	E-2-22	02072287	13 MAR 45	LUXEMBOURG
ROGERS, JAMES N. JR. S/SGT	599BS	397	E-1-49	15114943	25 DEC 44	LUXEMBOURG
ROSE, LYNN E. JR. S/SGT	599BS	397	H-6-60	17175887	23 DEC 44	LUXEMBOURG
SCHERER, NORMAN S. 1/LT	598BS	397	C-1-15	0-887158	23 DEC 44	LUXEMBOURG
SENART, BERNARD F. JR. 1/LT	599BS	397	B-9-4	0-687770	23 DEC 44	LUXEMBOURG
STANGLE, DONALD M. CAPT	598BS	397	H-16-13	0-025646	23 DEC 44	LUXEMBOURG
SWENSON, ERICK C. T/SGT	599BS	397	H-10-36	11063668	23 DEC 44	LUXEMBOURG
WATSON, HARRY H. S/SGT	599BS	397	E-5-34	35375624	23 DEC 44	LUXEMBOURG
WENBORG, GORDON H. 2/LT	509BS	397	B-7-45	0-777882	23 DEC 44	LUXEMBOURG
WILLIAMS, ROBERT D. SGT	598BS	397	D-5-24	35405881	23 DEC 44	LUXEMBOURG

Gravesite of General George S. Patton in foreground — Luxembourg American Cemetery and Memorial.

NETHERLANDS CEMETERY

Netherlands Cemetery the only American military cemetery in the Netherlands, lies in the village of Margraten, 6 miles east of Maastricht.

The tall memorial tower can be seen before reaching the site which covers 65 1/2 acres. From the cemetery entrance the visitor is led to the Court of Honor with its pool reflecting the tower. To the right and left, respectively, are the visitors' building and the museum containing three large engraved maps with texts depicting the military operations of the American Armed Forces.

Stretching along the sides of the court are the two Walls of the Missing on which are recorded the names of 1,722 who gave their lives in the service of their Country, but who rest in unknown graves. Beyond the tower containing the chapel is the burial area, divided into 16 plots, where rest 8,301 of our military Dead, their headstones set in long curves. A wide tree-lined mall leads to the flag staff which crowns the crest.

The light fixture in the chapel, and the altar candelabra and flowerbowl were presented by the Government of the Netherlands and by the local Provincial administration.

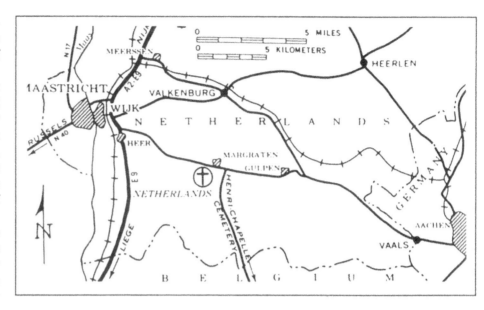

HISTORY

Three months after successfully landing on the beaches of Normandy, Allied forces had advanced farther than they had thought possible. By mid-September 1944, the U.S. First Army had crossed Luxembourg, captured Liege, Belgium; reached the German frontier near Aachen; and entered the Netherlands near Masstricht. The U.S. third Army sweeping across France on the right had reached the Moselle River and made contact with the U.S. Seventh Army driving northward from southern France. The British Second Army on the left had liberated Brussels and Antwerp, as the Canadian First Army kept pace with it along the coast liberating Ostend and Bruges; both Armies then found themselves astride the Netherlands frontier.

At this point, enemy defenses began to stabilize around the Siegfried Line, the heavily fortified cities in front of that line to the west, and the more easily defensible natural barriers provided by the numerous rivers and canals in the Netherlands to the east.

In an attempt to outflank the north end of the Siegfried Line, the Allies launched a combined airborne-ground assault along a narrow corridor across three major rivers (the Meuse, the Rhine and the Neder Rijn) and several canals, the success of which among other things depended heavily upon surprise. On 17 September 1944, elements of three divisions of the Allied First Airborne Army were landed by parachute and glider in column along the main road from Eindoven to Nijmegen to Arnhem, a distance of 64 miles from the starting point of the supporting British 30 Corps. Almost immediately, 30 Corps, consisting of one Armored and two Infantry Divisions, encountered stronger resistance than was anticipated. Therefore, its progress was much slower than planned.

Aided by air cover from the U.S. Eighth and Ninth Air Forces and the Royal Air Force, the landings on the drop ones were extraordinarily successful. In the Eindhoven area, the U.S. 101st Air-borne Division captured all bridges except one that was destroyed by the enemy. Contrary to plans, the supporting ground column did not reach Eindhoven until the second day and it was early on the third day before the destroyed bridge was replaced.

South of Nijmegen, the U.S. 82nd Airborne Division quickly seized the bridge over the Maas (Meuse) River. It was not until the 4th day (20 September), however, that the bridge over the Waal (Rhine) River was captured and not until the 5th day that all defenders were cleared from the area and ground troops were able to cross. The most important bridge of all over the Neder Rijn (lower Rhine) was still ten miles away.

Enemy reaction at Arnhem was swift and telling, as it quickly separated the battalion of the British 1st Airborne Division that had seized the north end of the Arnhm bridge from the remainder of the division and encircled the drop zones west of the city. Harsh weather further complicated the problem by preventing the cutoff battalion from being supported from the air. On the 6th day, a Polish Parachute Brigade made a valiant but unsuccessful attempt to reinforce it. Even when ground troops arrived on 23 September (the 7th day), all attempts to send reinforcements north of the river failed. After dark on 25 September, the battalion's remnants, less than one-quarter of those who had landed, were evacuated to the south bank.

Allied progress during the next three months was slow as opposition stiffened in all areas. The British Second Army concentrated on widening the sides of the Nijmegen corridor, while the Canadian First Army performed the difficult task of opening the Schelde estuary, so that the port of Antwerp could begin to operate on 28 November and ease the logistical burden. The main Allied offensive effort during this period was shifted to the center of the enemy defenses. There, the U.S. First Army with strong air support from the U.S. Ninth Air Force, broke through the Siegfried Line and encircled Aachen which surrendered on 21 October. The U.S. Ninth Army, which had been organized at Brest in Brittany, was shifted from the U.S. First Army's right flank to its left. Together, the two Armies continued the assault to the Roer River. On their right, the U.S. Third Army and the U.S. Seventh Army, with the French First Army on the extreme right, made substantial gains toward the German frontier.

Suddenly on 16 December 1944, the Allied advance was interrupted as the enemy launched its final major counteroffensive of the war in the Ardennes, followed by a second assault in Alsace to the south. By the end of January 1945, these offensives were halted and all ground retaken. The Allies then resumed their advance, which was planned in two stages. The first stage was to clear all enemy units west of the Rhine, the second was to invade Germany itself.

The advance to the Rhine in the north was scheduled to begin on 8 February 1945, with the Canadian First Army attacking to the southeast, followed in two days by a converging attack to the northeast by the U.S. Ninth and First Armies. When the V Corps of U.S. First Army seized control of the upstream dams of the Roer on 10 February, it discovered that the enemy had wrecked the discharge valves the evening before. The resultant heavy flow of water halted the attack there for two weeks.

At 0245 hours on 23 February, following a short but intensive air and artillery bombardment, the U. S. Ninth Army lowered its assault boats into the swirling waters and began to cross the Roer River before the flood waters had completely subsided. Despite heavy enemy artillery fire, Julich was captured on the first day, with the support of fighters and medium bombers of the U. S. Ninth Air Force.

By 25 February, all four corps of the U.S. Ninth Army had crossed the Roer and were advancing. As the advance turned northward, the armored units were committed. By 1 March 1945, the industrial city of Monchen-Gladbach had been captured. It was the largest German city taken to date. Now the advance became a race to destroy as many units as possible before they could retreat across the Rhine. Despite constant harassment by our aircraft, the enemy was able to demolish all bridges across the Rhine. On 10 March, the entire west bank of the Rhine from Dusseldorf northward was in Allied hands.

The major assault crossing of the Rhine occurred on 23-24 March, when the U.S. Ninth Army crossed at Rheinberg, a city it had captured on 6 March. Advancing Allied armies by-passed the northern Netherlands, encircled the Ruhr, then pursued the retreating enemy throughout Germany and Austria. All enemy forces in Europe surrendered on 8 May 1945.

Mourning Woman — Netherlands American Cemetery and Memorial.

Netherlands American Cemetery with the memorial in the background.

NETHERLANDS CEMETERY

Name & Rank	Unit	Gp	Pl-Row-Gr	Number	Date of Death	Cemetery
BETZ, WILLIAM R. 2/LT	452BS	322	16-I-7	0-790934	17 MAY 43	NETHERLANDS
BURNS, JOHN H. 2/LT	452BS	322	B-19-11	0-731019	17 MAY 43	NETHERLANDS
CONVERSE, WILLIAM CAPT	452BS	322	A-8-29	0-725585	17 MAY 43	NETHERLANDS
DONALDSON, MELVIN E. FLT/O	450BS	322	O-17-5	T-132581	14 MAR 45	NETHERLANDS
DWYER, WARREN J, SGT	450BS	322	M-20-17	38297912	11 APR 45	NETHERLANDS
GARRARD, CURTIS F. S/SGT	452BS	322	G-21-8	14061410	24 MAR 45	NETHERLANDS
HAGETTER, EDWARD K. S/SGT	452BS	322	J-9-9	19016978	17 MAY 43	NETHERLANDS
HARTENSTEIN, ROBERT E. 2/LT	452BS	322	E-3-18	0-557204	28 NOV 44	NETHERLANDS
HAWKINS, WILLIAM R. 2/LT	452BS	322	C-4-1	0-557294	28 NOV 44	NETHERLANDS
JONES, JOSEPH A. 1/LT	450BS	322	O-21-7	0-791700	17 MAY 43	NETHERLANDS
MAC DOUGALL, RALPH H. SGT	452BS	322	P-22-3	11037593	17 MAY 43	NETHERLANDS
MARSHALL, DAROLD E. SGT	450BS	322	O-3-1	18202810	14 MAR 45	NETHERLANDS
MISCHK, JOSEPH M. S/SGT	450BS	322	L-14-19	31332552	23 FEB 45	NETHERLANDS
MUNSON, ROBERT B. JR. SGT	450BS	322	M-1-3	17092179	14 MAR 45	NETHERLANDS
NASH, JOHN L. S/SGT	452BS	322	B-19-10	11038388	17 MAY 43	NETHERLANDS
NORTON, JAMES A. JR. 2/LT	452BS	322	P-16-5	0-792300	17 MAY 43	NETHERLANDS
RESWEBER, ELLIS J. 1/LT	452BS	322	H-9-10	0-791727	17 MAY 43	NETHERLANDS
ROSFELD, DAVID V. SGT	450BS	322	L-7-20	38485284	14 MAR 45	NETHERLANDS
TAGGART, LYLE A. 2/LT	450BS	322	L-7-8	0-780073	23 FEB 45	NETHERLANDS
VANDERGRIFT, JACK E. 1/LT	452BS	322	M-17-14	0-663107	17 MAY 43	NETHERLANDS
WALLERSTEIN, EDWARD 2/LT	450BS	322	M-16-3	0-746774	23 FEB 45	NETHERLANDS
WOLFE, RICHARD O. 1/LT	452BS	322	A-8-21	0-791745	17 MAY 43	NETHERLANDS
ZEINDENFELD, ALVIN X. 1/LT	452BS	322	O-22-17	0-662330	17 MAY 43	NETHERLANDS
AULENBACH, AARON A. S/SGT	456BS	323	0-2-1	33230201	03 APR 45	NETHERLANDS
HOFFMAN, JOHN C. 2/LT	455BS	323	D-2-5	0-721750	25 FEB 45	NETHERLANDS
KITCHELL, JAMES R. S/SGT	456BS	323	H-16-13	36054408	03/NOV 43	NETHERLANDS
LEIBENSPRERGER, RUSSELL S/SGT	455BS	323	D-1-22	33232612	26 DEC 44	NETHERLANDS
PEGUES, ROBERT A. SGT	455BS	323	C-14-7	18201930	25 FEB 45	NETHERLANDS
REESE, HALMYTH C. 2/LT	453BS	323	A-14-26	0-672201	26 MAR 44	NETHERLANDS
SCOTT, PAUL R. SGT	453BS	323	J-16-1	35662878	26 MAR 44	NETHERLANDS
SUNDBERG, ALEX E. S/SGT	453BS	323	K-18-3	39309115	26 MAR 44	NETHERLANDS
VIOLAND, BASIL G. SGT	456BS	323	N-11-4	35009973	03 APR 45	NETHERLANDS
CHAPMAN, CARL F. JR CAPT	497BS	344	L-3-1	0-659663	23 FEB 45	NETHERLANDS
COMSTOCK, JACK B 1/LT	494BS	344	D-4-3	0-669680	23 SEPT 44	NETHERLANDS
DAVIES, JERALD M. CAPT	495BS	344	G-18-1	0-024607	10 SEPT 45	NETHERLANDS
DIMITRE, JOHN J. 2/LT	495BS	344	B-6-5	02079316	31 MAY 45	NETHERLANDS
DUMM, JAMES J. JR S/SGT	495BS	344	H-2-5	13083120	31 MAY 45	NETHERLANDS
FOLSOM, ROBERT H S/SGT	494BS	344	A-15-30	07001301	02 MAR 45	NETHERLANDS
GILROY, JAMES S SGT	495BS	344	M-14-2	36457707	24 FEB 45	NETHERLANDS

Name & Rank	Unit	Gp	Pl-Row-Gr	Number	Date of Death	Cemetery
HERNDON, J. P. T/SGT	497BS	344	O-21-1	18005969	23 FEB 45	NETHERLANDS
JOHNSON, ALGOTH W. S/SGT	494BS	344	P-5-14	31103116	23 SEPT 44	NETHERLANDS
JONES, WILLIAM R. 1/LT	497BS	344	J-3-12	0-760860	14 FEB 45	NETHERLANDS
MONAHAN, EDWARD J. SGT	495BS	344	H-17-22	12144326	14 FEB 45	NETHERLANDS
NEAL, MAURICE J. 2/LT	494BS	344	C-8-24	0-765712	23 SEPT 44	NETHERLANDS
REITZ, WILLIAM CAPT	496BS	344	A-12-15	0-429852	23 SEPT 44	NETHERLANDS
ROBINSON, RICHARD E. 1/LT	495BS	344	D-9-31	0-822813	31 MAY 45	NETHERLANDS
WILLIAMSON, W. T. S/SGT	497BS	344	L-4-22	18083363	23 FEB 45	NETHERLANDS
ZUEST, HARRY W. 2/LT	495BS	344	K-21-20	02068152	14 FEB 45	NETHERLANDS
CROSSWELL, ALLEN J. S/SGT	555BS	386	I-1-2	31103360	09 AUG 43	NETHERLANDS
CUTHBERTSON, JAMES F. SGT	553BS	386	B-17-6	13077806	30 JUL 43	NETHERLANDS
HERCKER, JOSEPH H. S/SGT	554BS	386	B-17-15	33790960	03 APR 45	NETHERLANDS
ROBERTS, RAYMOND C. FLT/O	555BS	386	M-12-9	T-120450	13 DEC 43	NETHERLANDS
THORNTON, CHARLES V. MAJ	555BS	386	I-8-7	0-399507	22 FEB 44	NETHERLANDS
WARMUTH, ARNOLD P. JR. 2/LT	559BS	387	O-20-2	0-738049	02 MAR 44	NETHERLANDS
WESOLOWSKI, EDWARD V. S/SGT	558BS	387	H-9-1	32842739	14 FEB 45	NETHERLANDS
WHITE, JAMES W. SGT	559BS	387	M-12-3	38207065	02 MAR 44	NETHERLANDS
WILLETT, RALPH A. T/SGT	558BS	387	L-4-21	37479373	08 MAY 45	NETHERLANDS
YOUNG, ROBERT K. 2/LT	556BS	387	G-13-24	0-721899	10 MAY 45	NETHERLANDS
ANDERSON, ERNEST L 1/LT	558BS	387	P-4-11	0-731784	21 AUG 43	NETHERLANDS
FITZGERALD, ROBERT J. T/SGT	557BS	387	N-3-11	12050875	21 MAR 45	NETHERLANDS
GOBER, JOHN H. S/SGT	559BS	387	B-12-5	18136266	02 MAR 44	NETHERLANDS
HELINE, CARL W. 2/LT	557BS	387	J-2-16	0-721070	14 FEB 45	NETHERLANDS
POWERS, WILLIAM B. JR. T/SGT	558BS	387	N-18-12	11086882	31 AUG 43	NETHERLANDS
SMITH, WAYNE R. 1/LT	558BS	387	K-2-14	0-760706	14 FEB 45	NETHERLANDS
STEVENSON, LOUIS C. 2/LT	558BS	387	C-10-2	0-742219	31 AUG 43	NETHERLANDS
STURM, ROBERT P. 1/LT	558BS	387	G-13-1	0-709984	08 MAY 45	NETHERLANDS
TAYLOR, ROBERT L. 1/LT	558BS	387	L-13-2	0-700576	25 JAN 45	NETHERLANDS
HARSIN, HAROLD E. 1/LT	575BS	391	N-14-7	0-855860	24 FEB 45	NETHERLANDS
RANSOM, WILLIAM V. FLT/O	574BS	391	J-1-15	T-128665	25 JAN 45	NETHERLANDS
ROCHEFORT, WILLIAM H. FLT/O	574BS	391	I-10-7	T-131618	10 FEB 45	NETHERLANDS
SILVERSTON, ROBERT L. SGT	573BS	391	H-10-4	36557244	10 FEB 45	NETHERLANDS
WILLIAMS, ROBERT P. SGT	574BS	391	I-11-7	34801536	25 JAN 45	NETHERLANDS
BASSETT, GEORGE S. 2/LT	587BS	394	I-1-3	02067266	23 JUL 45	NETHERLANDS
COON, CARL W. SGT	584BS	394	D-15-29	16149828	14 FEB 45	NETHERLANDS
CLARK, ANDREW F. JR 2/LT	587BS	394	J-20-21	0-720438	15 MAY 45	NETHERLANDS
EATON, NORMAN H. 2/LT	587BS	394	N-11-8	0-836747	15 NAY 45	NETHERLANDS
FOER, BERNARD W. SGT	585BS	394	I-9-6	32390691	18 JUL 45	NETHERLANDS
FORD, ROBERT L. S/LT	586BS	394	L-8-4	02029375	18 SEPT 45	NETHERLANDS
HARRISON, JAMES C. 1/LT	584BS	394	C-20-29	0-739463	21 NOV 44	NETHERLANDS
JOYCE, WILLIAM P. 2/LT	587BS	394	0-7-10	02062511	08-APR 45	NETHERLANDS

Name & Rank	Unit	Gp	Pl-Row-Gr	Number	Date of Death	Cemetery
SCAFIDE, SALVATORE C. CPL	585BS	394	H-7-8	32441775	19 JUL 45	NETHERLANDS
DRYDEN, PHILIP C. 1/LT	599BS	397	H-8-14	0-812956	03 JAN 45	NETHERLANDS
EPPS, WILLIAM E. T/SGT	596BS	397	D-3-28	38449367	23 DEC 44	NETHERLANDS
POULSON, GLENN W. 2/LT	599BS	397	N-21-1	0-788083	08 APR 45	NETHERLANDS
STARKEY, ROBERT R. 1/LT	599BS	397	N-21-16	0-715840	08 APR 45	NETHERLANDS
THOMAS, JOSEPH V. L. S/SGT	599BS	397	0-22-6	39272378	08 APR 45	NETHERLANDS

NORMANDY CEMETERY

Normandy Cemetery is situated on a cliff overlooking Omaha Beach and the English Channel, just east of St. Laurent-sur-Mer and northwest of Bayeus in Colleville-sur-Mer, 170 miles west of Paris.

The cemetery site, at the north end of its 1/2 mile access road, covers 172 1/2 acres and contains the graves of 9,386 of our military Dead, most of whom gave their lives in the landings and ensuing operations. On the walls of the semicircular garden on the east side of the memorial are inscribed the names of 1,557 of our Missing who rest in unknown graves.

The memorial consists of a semicircular colonnade with a loggia at each containing large maps and narratives of the military operations, at the center is the bronze "Spirit of American Youth." Two orientation tables, which overlook the beach, depict the landings in Normandy and the artificial harbor established here. Facing west at the memorial, one sees in the foreground the reflecting pool; beyond is the burial area with the circular chapel and, at the far end, the granite statues representing the United States and France.

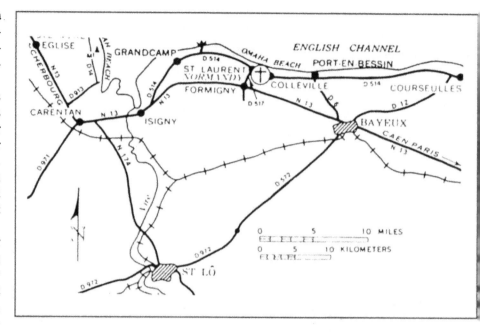

HISTORY

Many months of planning and preparation preceded the 6 June 1944 D-Day landings in Normandy. Beginning in March 1944, Allied air forces disrupted transportation between the Seine and Loire Rivers and conducted strategic air bombardment deep into enemy territory in an attempt to keep the German air force occupied and on the defensive and to isolate the landing areas.

On 6 June 1944 during the early morning hours of darkness, three airborne divisions (the British 6th and the U.S. 82nd and 101st) were dropped to the rear of the search area to cover deployment of the seaborne assault forces. Simultaneously, Allied naval forces swept the English Channel of mines and preceded the assault vessels to the landing areas. At 0630 hours, under cover of intense naval and air bombardment, six U.S. British and Canadian divisions began landing on Utah, Omaha, Gold, Juno and Sword beaches in what was to be the greatest amphibious assault in recorded history.

The U.S. 4th Division landed at Utah Beach and pushed rapidly inland to joint the airborne division. The early success and extraordinarily light casualties on Utah Beach contrasted sharply with the difficulties of the U.S. 1st and 29th Divisions on Omaha Beach to the east, where the enemy was resisting with every device and weapon at his disposal. Its terrain alone was a major obstacle. Instead of sloping gently from the high ground to the rear, the beach area terminated in steep sandy bluffs. Troops had to cross an open area varying in width from a few yards at each end to about 200 yards in the center, and then attack up the steep bluffs to the plateau where the Normandy American Cemetery now stands. The only concealment available was patches of tall marsh grass. Fighting was bitter and casualties heavy. Nevertheless, before D-Day was over, the U.S. 1st Division took the high ground on which the cemetery stands.

Further to the east on Gold, Juno and Sword landing beaches, the British and Canadian divisions forged steadily ahead. Within a week, under the cover of continuous naval gunfire and air support, the individual beachheads were linked together. Temporary anchorage's and artificial harbors were constructed off the beachhead area during this period by sinking ships and anchoring prefabricated concrete caissons to the channel floor, facilitating the unloading of troops and supplies.

Rapidly, the Allied armies increased in size and strength. On 26 June, Americans freed Cherbourg; on 9 July, British and

Spirit of American Youth Rising from the Waves — Normandy American Cemetery and Memorial.

Canadians fought their way into Caen; and on 18 July, Americans took St. Lo. Preceded by a paralyzing air bombardment on 25 July, the U.S. First Army stormed out of the beachhead area. Coutances was liberated three days later and, within a week, the recently activated U.S. Third Army cleared Avranches and was advancing toward Paris on a broad front.

Top: Memorial Garden with Tablets of the Missing in background — Normandy American American Cemetery and Memorial. Bottom: The Normandy American Cemetery with the memorial in the foreground and the burial area in the background.

NORMANDY CEMETERY

Name & Rank	Unit	Gp	Pl-Row-Gr	Number	Date of Death	Cemetery
ALLEN, RUSSELL E. T/SGT	452BS	322	I-16-23	35367217	30 JUL 44	NORMANDY
AMOR, JAMES P. SGT	451BS	322	B-1-33	1469762	25 MAR 44	NORMANDY
BEKAERT, GERARD J. S/SGT	451BS	322	I-1-21	12035149	06 AUG 44	NORMANDY
BENTLEY, THEODORE N. SGT	452BS	322	B-19-24	15098544	25 MAR 44	NORMANDY
BINGHAM, ROBERT P 1/LT	452BS	322	A-22-39	0-672306	08 JUL 44	NORMANDY
BLACKSTONE, ROBERT H. S/SGT	451BS	322	C-18-14	32479418	08 JUL 44	NORMANDY
BONNETT, HOY C. JR. 1/LT	451BS	322	B-12-28	0-664504	29 FEB 44	NORMANDY
CARLSON, CLAYTON C. 2/LT	452BS	322	B-20-33	0-741464	25 MAR 44	NORMANDY
CLOSE, RAYMOND M. SGT	451BS	322	B-6-23	15074874	08 JUL 44	NORMANDY
CONSIDINE, WILFRED B. S/SGT	452BS	322	J-21-28	11054538	25 MAR 44	NORMANDY
CORONES, JAMES G. 2/LT	452BS	322	B-5-42	0-807158	13 JUN 44	NORMANDY
DAVISON, ELLIS H. 1/LT	450BS	322	C-5-26	0-670512	08 JUL 44	NORMANDY
GUILIANO, JAMES L. T/SGT	450BS	322	J-27-32	32340160	09 SEPT 43	NORMANDY
HEISER, GEORGE E. T/SGT	451BS	322	H-3-31	06991370	06 AUG 44	NORMANDY
HILL, GEORGE R. T/SGT	451BS	322	B-23-35	13092901	08 JUL 44	NORMANDY
HOLMES, LARRY L. 1/LT	452BS	322	J-24-19	0-671022	13 JUN 44	NORMANDY
JONES, CLAUDE B. 1/LT	451BS	322	D-3-34	0-530745	08 JUL 44	NORMANDY
LANNIN, WILLIAM B. FLT/O	452BS	322	B-14-5	T-190616	25 MAR 44	NORMANDY
LEMMOND, JAMES W. 1/LT	451BS	322	C-22-8	0-668014	08 JULY 44	NORMANDY
MATTHEWS, FONTAINE M. 1/LT	452BS	322	D-4-45	0-732879	23 NOV 43	NORMANDY
MAY, JOHN V. T/SGT	451BS	322	B-14-8	11041187	05 NOV 43	NORMANDY
McGLOCKLIN, LYLE G. 1/LT	450BS	322	C-13-25	0-732562	09 MAY 44	NORMANDY
MOON, GEORGE R. T/SGT	451BS	322	D-1-34	19022116	08 JULY 44	NORMANDY
MOORE, JESSE M. S/SGT	451BS	322	H-17-13	14083860	06 AUG 44	NORMANDY
MORIN, RAYMOND J. T/SGT	449BS	322	F-19-16	31127019	12 AUG 44	NORMANDY
OLSEN, EUGENE M. S/SGT	452BS	322	A-11-32	13053898	24 MAR 44	NORMANDY
PUSTELNIK, GEORGE H. SGT	452BS	322	I-27-5	36121684	13 JUNE 44	NORMANDY
ROLAND, ROBERT L. 1/LT	452BS	322	A-5-32	0-678574	25 MAR 44	NORMANDY
ROSNER, ELMER T/SGT	452BS	322	B-7-41	18044426	08 JULY 44	NORMANDY
SHOOP, JAMES M. 2/LT	452BS	322	B-19-42	0-815568	13 JUN 44	NORMANDY
SMITH, GEORGE J. 1/LT	451BS	322	G-20-28	0-672473	06 AUG 44	NORMANDY
SPENCER, RAYMOND W. FLT/O	452BS	322	B-20-B	T-120456	08 JULY 44	NORMANDY
STARK, WILLIAM F. S/SGT	449BS	322	C-8-37	18074157	12 AUG 44	NORMANDY
TATE, ROBERT S. FLT/O	452BS	322	A-15-5	T-120349	25 MAR 44	NORMANDY
THOMPSON, JOE E. JR. 1/LT	452BS	322	C-1-47	0-672486	08 JULY 44	NORMANDY
WATERS, RICHARD J. 1/LT	450BS	322	A-13-42	0-886142	08 JULY 44	NORMANDY
WINSTEAD, JAMES W. S/SGT	451BS	322	B-5-19	14151496	08 JULY 44	NORMANDY
CLARK, ROLAND E. S/SGT	453BS	323	B-12-8	39250858	31 JULY 43	NORMANDY
COURSEN, GEORGE H. S/SGT	454BS	323	B-21-17	06904143	23 NOV 45	NORMANDY
EDWARDS, GEORGE P. 1/LT	453BS	323	A-18-15	0-791803	31 JULY 43	NORMANDY

Name & Rank	Unit	Gp	Pl-Row-Gr	Number	Date of Death	Cemetery
HOLTHUSEN, ADOLF C. S/SGT	456BS	323	A-15-19	32221666	29 JUNE 44	NORMANDY
LIPSCOMB, JOHN P. CAPT	453BS	323	B-12-7	0-438451	31 JULY 43	NORMANDY
WEBB, DAVID W. 1/LT	454BS	323	A-23-41	0-525083	23 NOV 43	NORMANDY
WHITMAN, WILLIAM S. 2/LT	455BS	323	F-13-34	0-687789	09 SEPT 44	NORMANDY
BILLINGS, SHERRARD II S/SGT	496BS	344	A-19-25	31093591	10 JUN 44	NORMANDY
DYE, JOHN W. 2/LT	496BS	344	B-6-17	0-693651	27 APR 44	NORMANDY
GARLICK, ROBERT JR. S/SGT	496BS	344	A-8-10	31078257	27 APR 44	NORMANDY
GISAVAGE, JOSEPH G. S/SGT	496BS	344	A-10-7	1221966	10 JUN 44	NORMANDY
LOBB, LEONARD C. 2/LT	495BS	344	E-23-32	0-815727	11 MAY 44	NORMANDY
PORTER, MARSHALL H. S/SGT	496BS	344	A-18-25	3128164	27 APR 44	NORMANDY
SAVKO, JOSEPH 1/LT	496BS	344	I-15-28	0-801964	27 APR 44	NORMANDY
SMITH, EVERETT T. 2/LT	495BS	344	A-21-42	37180054	23 APR 44'	NORMANDY
BEYL, ROBERT N. SGT	554BS	386	B-10-12	34336613	31 JUL 44	NORMANDY
BRIGGS, FREDERICK O. 1/LT	553BS	386	G-12-30	0-813311	28 JUL 44	NORMANDY
BRUSMAN, JACK P. S/SGT	553BS	386	B-6-18	15068245	05 NOV 43	NORMANDY
CALDWELL, WILMA T. JR. 2/LT	554BS	386	B-4-23	0-521569	22 AUG 43	NORMANDY
COFFEY, WILLIAM J. JR. 2/LT	552BS	386	D-10-41	0-731147	09 SEPT 43	NORMANDY
COYLE, THEODORE P. S/SGT	555BS	386	A-8-19	13046545	1 JUL 48	NORMANDY
DANFORTH, STEPHEN M. 1/LT	552BS	386	B-18-8	0-793075	09 SEPT 43	NORMANDY
DORTON, JOHN L. S/SGT	554BS	386	D-17-40	35285622	10 FEB 44	NORMANDY
FAITH, RICHARD R. T/SGT	554BS	386	A-14-39	13087676	10 FEB 44	NORMANDY
KIRK, LEO W. S/SGT	555BS	386	J-27-5	12035105	18 JUL 44	NORMANDY
LEHMAN, CLAYTON E. S/SGT	554BS	386	B-10-24	34209974	31 JUL 44	NORMANDY
LODGE, WARREN F. JR. 2/LT	555BS	386	B-17-39	0-816511	12 JUN 44	NORMANDY
LOPEZ, ADOLFO A. JR. T/SGT	555BS	386	A-22-41	14081746	18 JUL 44	NORMANDY
McGONIGLE, LEON F. S/SGT	555BS	386	B-8-41	33084199	12 JUN 44	NORMANDY
MILLER, CHARLES A. 1/LT	555BS	386	B-16-28	0-671060	05 FEB 44	NORMANDY
MITSTIFER, DAYTON B. FLT/O	554BS	386	D-5-39	T-186567	10 FEB 44	NORMANDY
NEWELL, WILLIAM R. SGT	552BS	386	B-7-32	16035979	25 SEPT 43	NORMANDY
PARSONS, FLOYD L. 1/LT	552BS	386	D-18-34	0-744939	16 AUG 44	NORMANDY
RAY, WILLIAM C. 1/LT	554BS	386	A-1-21	0-672867	17 JULY 44	NORMANDY
SOLOMON, CHARLES L. SGT	553BS	386	D-25-40	12062622	05 NOV 43	NORMANDY
SWANSON, FRANKLIN E. SGT	554BS	386	B-9-6	12139321	06 AUG 44	NORMANDY
VERMETTE, ARTHUR J. S/SGT	552BS	386	I-26-10	16067443	27 SEPT 43	NORMANDY
WHITEHEAD, JACK E. T/SGT	552BS	386	B-13-17	19029513	09 SEPT 43	NORMANDY
WILLIAMSON, RAY D. CAPT	553BS	386	B-7-33	0-727821	05 NOV 43	NORMANDY
CHRISTLEY, CURTIS L S/SGT	556BS	387	B-4-41	33164439	29 NOV 43	NORMANDY
DAVIS, IRA G. 2/LT	558BS	387	E-8-3	0-547542	08 JUN 44	NORMANDY
HANNA, DANNIEL R. III 1/LT	556BS	387	E-11-33	0-738382	12 MAY 44	NORMANDY
HUNTER, GAIL R. S/SGT	558BS	387	E-4-15	37109559	08 JUN 44	NORMANDY
KOURY, MICHAEL G. 1/LT	556BS	387	D-5-12	0-729981	15 FEB 44	NORMANDY
McDONALD, JOHN J. JR. 1/LT	558BS	387	G-23-19	0-797039	08 JUN 44	NORMANDY
MICHAEL, HOWARD E. S/SGT	558BS	387	A-13-43	39549959	28 AUG 44	NORMANDY

Name & Rank	Unit	Gp	Pl-Row-Gr	Number	Date of Death	Cemetery
PEQUIGNOT, WILLIAM J. S/SGT	558BS	387	G-3-17	13057193	08 JUN 44	NORMANDY
RESTAINO, AUGUST T/SGT	559BS	387	A-15-30	13010670	02 SEPT 43	NORMANDY
ROOT, JOHN D. CAPT	558BS	387	J-10-14	0-856946	08 JUN 44	NORMANDY
RYAN, ANDREW 1/LT	559BS	387	D-8-45	0-794055	02 SPET 43	NORMANDY
SOMMERS, FRANKLIN W. 2/LT	559BS	387	A-14-32	0-742377	02 SEPT 43	NORMANDY
VOSBURGHM WILLIAM F. 1/LT	559BS	387	D-15-41	0-793205	02 SEPT 43	NORMANDY
BERNZEN, FRANK JR, 1/LT	573BS	391	D-3-42	0-738335	19 MAR 44	NORMANDY
BROWN, GALE F. S/SGT	573BS	391	D-16-34	36448267	19 MAR 44	NORMANDY
CULSHAW, JOHN R. S/SGT	573BS	391	I-26-17	33429297	28 JUL 44	NORMANDY
GRACE, THADDEUS H. T/SGT	573BS	391	D-24-40	34331037	19 MAR 44	NORMANDY
GROVE, EDWARD N. PVT	573BS	391	A-11-22	0-684328	05 JUL 44	NORMANDY
HARTMAN, LOUIS E. 1/LT	573BS	391	A-14-14	0-684328	05 JUL 44	NORMANDY
HILL, JOHN D. 2/LT	573BS	391	A-16-42	0-692789	19 MAR 44	NORMANDY
KOHLER, JOHN F. 1/LT	573BS	391	B-11-43	0-746894	13 AUG 44	NORMANDY
KREFT, ANDRE F. S/SGT	575BS	391	B-19-22	12057415	27 APR 44	NORMANDY
LA PLANTE, JOHN F. S/SGT	573BS	391	A-11-4	11035865	19 MAR 44	NORMANDY
MARTEL, ERNEST T/SGT	575BS	391	J-26-14	31150127	05 JUL 44	NORMANDY
PAVINSKI, ADOLPH L. S/SGT	573BS	391	J-17-28	06995380	05 JUL 44	NORMANDY
PETERSON, KENNETH D. S/SGT	575BS	391	C-7-17	37220369	07 JUN 44	NORMANDY
ROLLINGS, WILLIAM S. T/SGT	573BS	391	B-2-19	33499791	28 JUL 44	NORMANDY
RUGG, EARL J. 2/LT	574BS	391	D-1-47	0-757291	07 AUG 44	NORMANDY
STEVENSON, ANDREW R. S/SGT	572BS	391	B-14-17	32787720	18 AR 44	NORMANDY
YOUNG, GLEN L. SGT	573BS	391	B-4-34	37563389	13 AUG 44	NORMANDY
CARMOSINO, SAMUEL J. PFC	584BS	394	D-17-45	33271100	21 APR 44	NORMANDY
DE BELL, JOHN A. FLT/0	587BS	394	A-16-31	T-002045	21 APR 44	NORMANDY
FREEMAN, STUART E. 1/LT	584BS	394	D-7-45	0-801548	21 APR 44	NORMANDY
HEALY, PATRICK J. 2/LT	585BS	394	D-14-3	0-699166	12 JUN 44	NORMANDY
JONES, JAMES D. 1/LT	585BS	394	A-8-14	0-739438	12 JUNE 44	NORMANDY
KUBALA, THEODORE E. 1/LT	587BS	394	A-7-40	0-803224	21 APR 44	NORMANDY
LOWELL, BENJAMIN W. 2/LT	585BS	394	D-19-41	0-750805	07 AUG 44	NORMANDY
McGREGOR, JACK M. 1/LT	585BS	394	F-13-32	0-026324	02 AUG 44	NORMANDY
NOELTING, HAROLD L. S/SGT	584BS	394	B-22-21	36732833	21 SEPT 44	NORMANDY
SJOLANDER, LLOYD E. S/SGT	585BS	394	C-16-17	17024955	12 JUN 44	NORMANDY
SWEET, HAROLD S. SGT	585BS	394	C-10-4	06804805	07 AUG 44	NORMANDY
TRUMAN, HARLOW M. 2/LT	585BS	394	B-19-13	0-816618	07 AUG 44	NORMANDY
ARMSTRONG, DONALD B. T/SGT	524BS	397	A-16-3	35467488	03 SEPT 43	NORMANDY
HELLSTROM, LEONARD L. 1/LT	598BS	397	B-8-34	0-809802	10 AUG 44	NORMANDY
ROEBUCK, HAROLD M. T/SGT	598BS	397	G-3-26	06999923	07 JULY 44	NORMANDY

THE WALL OF THE MISSING

Name & Rank	Unit	Gp		Number	Date of Death	Cemetery
BAGGETT, JULIAN F. T/SGT	558BS	387	WALL	18064552	25 FEB 44	NETHERLANDS
BAILEY, EDWARD F. SGT	587BS	394	WALL	12189177	06 JUN 44	CAMBRIDGE
BAMBERGER, LOUIS J. 1/LT	453BS	323	WALL	0-741327	20 MAY 44	CAMBRIDGE
BASALDU, JOSE M. SGT	452BS	322	WALL	18102457	17 MAY 43	CAMBRIDGE
BECKER, CHARLES P. S/SGT	558BS	387	WALL	32279560	25 FEB 44	NETHERLANDS
BELOTE, JAMES W. T/SGT	452BS	322	WALL	20410212	17 MAY 43	CAMBRIDGE
BIEZIS, STEPHEN V. 2/LT	575BS	391	WALL	0-824081	24 DEC 45	HENRI - CHAPELLE
BILLINGS, FRANK E. SGT	454BS	323	WALL	37419477	20 MAY 44	NORMANDY
BLEAKER, LOUIS 1/LT	453BS	323	WALL	0-732801	11 APR 44	CAMBRIDGE
BOOTH, DWIGHT K. 2/LT	450BS	322	WALL	02070890	16 APR 45	NETHERLANDS
BOSACK, EDWARD R. SGT	494BS	344	WALL	131560542	19 NOV 44	HENRI - CHAPELLE
BOWAN, JOHN S/SGT	553BS	386	WALL	33362687	25 MAR 44	NORMANDY
BRAGG, PAUL W. S/SGT	553BS	386	WALL	15062935	30 JUL 43	NETHERLANDS
BRINSON, PHILIP L. S/SGT	450BS	322	WALL	34208695	09 SEPT 43	ARDENNES
BROWN, EDGAR H. 1/LT	556BS	387	WALL	0-662431	09 SEPT 43	ARDENNES
BUELL, HENRY E. 2/LT	552BS	386	WALL	0-738085	03 JUN 43	CAMBRIDGE
CALDWELL, JACK E COL	HQ	387	WALL	0-020743	12 APR 44	ARDENNES
CANTY, JOHN H. S/SGT	555BS	386	WALL	11072858	22 JUN 44	NORMANDY
CARPENTER, THOMAS J. S/SGT	455BS	323	WALL	14079896	13 DEC 43	CAMBRIDGE
CARUTHERS, THOMAS A. J. 2/LT	572BS	391	WALL	0-684273	18 APR 44	ARDENNES
CAVE, MARK W. SGT	495BS	344	WALL	18201748	29 MAY 45	LORRAINE
CHAMPLIN, JOHN B. 1/LT	450BS	322	WALL	0-662246	17 MAY 43	NETHERLANDS
CHANCE, WALTER E. SGT	455BS	323	WALL	32385103	13 DEC 43	NETHERLANDS
CHASWICK, JSOEPH R. 1/LT	452BS	322	WALL	0-731025	17 MAY 43	CAMBRIDGE
CHRISCO, EVERETT S/SGT	454BS	323	WALL	19113357	11 APR 44	CAMBRIDGE
CHROMY, JOHN H. T/SGT	454BS	323	WALL	16048005	20 MAY 44	ARDENNES
CLARK, JOHN W. S/SGT	552BS	386	WALL	32342451	03 JUN 43	CAMBRIDGE
COBURN, JOHN P. CAPT	558BS	387	WALL	0-729717	25 FEB 44	CAMBRIDGE
COE, ERNEST E. S/SGT	558BS	387	WALL	20848101	25 FEB 44	CAMBRIDGE
COLBRY, JOHN L. S/SGT	572BS	391	WALL	39022722	18 APR 44	ARDENNES
COLBY, LESLIE W. FLT/O	450BS	322	WALL	T-187567	09 SEPT 43	ARDENNES
COOK, WILLIAM P. 1/LT	559BS	397	WALL	0-749470	23 DEC 44	LUXEMBOURG
CRAINE, JOHN A. T/SGT	451BS	322	WALL	38119374	22 APR 44	CAMBRIDGE
CRANE, JACK CAPT	450BS	322	WALL	0-438487	17 MAY 43	CAMBRIDGE
CRAWFORD, GORDON P. SGT	558BS	387	WALL	20832066	25 FEB 44	NETHERLANDS
CURTIS, ROBERT E. 2/LT	553BS	386	WALL	0-744362	25 MAR 44	CAMBRIDGE
DAILEY, CLYDE T. 1/LT	558BS	387	WALL	0-669011	25 FEB 44	CAMBRIDGE
DALTON, JOE B. 2/LT	452BS	322	WALL	0-663488	17 MAY 43	CAMBRIDGE
DANISON, HOMER R. JR. 1/LT	439BS	319	WALL	0-661463	08 DEC 42	CAMBRIDGE
DAVIS, ROBET C. S/SGT	451BS	322	WALL	39829902	30 JUL 44	CAMBRIDGE
DEAN, CLARK T. CAPT	453BS	323	WALL	0-663242	20 MAY 44	ARDENESS
DENNY, LEO M. 1/LT	453BS	323	WALL	0-672770	11 APR 44	CAMBRIDGE
DETJENS, DALE C. 1/LT	574BS	391	WALL	0-705009	23 DEC 44	LUXEMBOURG
DONNELLY, EDWARD F. 2/LT	574BS	391	WALL	0-715739	23 DEC 44	HENRI - CHAPELLE
DORROH, TOM S. JR. 2/LT	439BS	319	WALL	0-727190	08 DEC 42	CAMBRIDGE
DOW, WILLIAM E. 1/LT	450BS	322	WALL	0-814668	16 APR 45	NETHERLANDS
ELLIOTT, CHARLES F. 2/LT	450BS	322	WALL	0-663498	17 MAY 43	NETHERLANDS
ENGELKING, OTTO B. 1/LT	572BS	391	WALL	0-670516	18 APR 44	ARDENNES
EVANS, ROBERT E. 2/LT	558BS	387	WALL	0-742145	25 FEB 44	CAMBRIDGE

Name & Rank	Unit	Gp		Number	Date of Death	Cemetery
FALLS, JOHN H. 1/LT	558BS	387	WALL	02044726	25 FEB 44	CAMBRIDGE
FARTHING, THAYER L. S/SGT	440BS	319	WALL	18128667	08 DEC 42	CAMBRIDGE
FEVOLD, MAURICE J. S/SGT	599BS	397	WALL	36656924	23 DEC 44	LUXEMBOURG
FORMICOLA, HARRY J. S/SGT	552BS	386	WALL	32238862	03 JUN 43	CAMBRIDGE
FOSTER, CHARLES R. S/SGT	453BS	323	WALL	35341475	11 APR 44	CAMBRIDGE
GATLIN, JAMES F. JR, 1/LT	575BS	391	WALL	0-685331	24 DEC 45	HENRI - CHAPELLE
GELORMO, DOMINIC A. S/SGT	558BS	387	WALL	33581094	15 JUN 44	CAMBRIDGE
GOLDSTEIN, MURRAY SGT	456BS	323	WALL	32420724	18 APR 44	ARDENNES
GRINDSTAFF, EARL T. 1/LT	455BS	323	WALL	0-667994	13 DEC 43	NETHERLANDS
GROSS, JOHN K. S/SGT	573BS	391	WALL	37316654	17 AUG 45	RHONE
GROTHOUSE, KENNETH J. S/SGT	451BS	322	WALL	15084995	29 FEB 44	CAMBRIDGE
HALL, DONALD D. T/SGT	552BS	386	WALL	17005722	03 JUN 43	CAMBRIDGE
HALL, JACK B. S/SGT	598BS	397	WALL	12072393	17 JUNE 44	CAMBRIDGE
HALNON, HOWARD J. 1/LT	556BS	387	WALL	0-732465	12 MAY 44	NORMANDY
HAMLEY, RAYMOND D. S/SGT	453BS	323	WALL	20213665	20 MAY 44	NORMANDY
HARBOUR, MARVIN L. SGT	450BS	322	WALL	18002633	17 MAY 43	NETHERLANDS
HARMES, FRANK M. 1/LT	456BS	323	WALL	0-663517	18 APR 44	ARDENNES
HASKINS, WARREN E. PVT	440BS	319	WALL	12030014	08 DEC 42	CAMBRIDGE
HAZLETT, GEORGE H. JR. 1/LT	555BS	386	WALL	0-794005	22 JUN 44	NORMANDY
HEAD, HOWARD S. S/SGT	558BS	387	WALL	37375502	25 FEB 44	CAMBRIDGE
HEARN, JAMES L. 1/LT	440BS	319	WALL	0-661485	08 DEC 42	CAMBRIDGE
HEATHER, WILLIAM J. JR. MAJ	453BS	323	WALL	0-727724	20 MAY 44	CAMBRISGE
HENRY, LEE A. T/SGT	553BS	386	WALL	13091170	29 MAY 44	ARDENNES
HERBERT, WILLIAM T. 2/LT	552BS	386	WALL	0-731185	03 JUN 43	CAMBRIDGE
HESSE, NORBERT F. S/SGT	556BS	387	WALL	37423489	09 SEPT 43	ARDENNES
HESSER, ROBERT R. 1/LT	599BS	397	WALL	0-693041	09 AUG 44	BRITTANY
HEWITT, ROBERT C. 1/LT	558BS	387	WALL	0-666039	29 MAY 44	NORMANDY
HODGES, JOHN H. 1/LT	558BS	387	WALL	0-732369	25 FEB 44	CAMBRIDGE
HOFFMAN, GUSTAVE E. CAPT	553BS	386	WALL	0-731584	29 MAY 44	ARDENNES
HOLLAND, JAMES J. CPL	439BS	319	WALL	32185125	08 DEC 42	CAMBRIDGE
HONEYMAN, ERIC M. SGT	599BS	397	WALL	39037489	23 DEC 44	LUXEMBOURG
HOWARD, ROBERT E. S/SGT	450BS	322	WALL	37664605	16 APR 45	NETHERLANDS
HUTCHINSON, JACK E. S/SGT	558BS	387	WALL	14040696	25 FEB 44	CAMBRIDGE
INSLEY, EDWIN G. T/SGT.	575BS	391	WALL	3064534	05 JUL 44	BRITTANY
JACK, JAMES M. 1/LT	558BS	387	WALL	0-680988	15 JUN 44	CAMBRIDGE
JACKSON, LEON R. 1/LT	453BS	323	WALL	0-671941	05 FEB 44	EPINAL
JANSING, ROBERT H. 1/LT	558BS	387	WALL	0-735791	25 FEB 44	CAMBRIDGE
JOHNSON, PAUL O. T/SGT	453BS	323	WALL	36198265	20 MAY 44	CAMBRIDGE
JORDAN, AUSTIN R. CAPT	451BS	322	WALL	0-664613	22 APR 44	CAMBRIDGE
KEEFER, RICHARD G. T/SGT	453BS	323	WALL	13087561	20 MAY 44	ARDENNES
KEEHLEY, JOHN F. FLT/O	497BS	344	WALL	T-061635	06 JUN 44	NORMANDY
KEGG, HARRISON E. S/SGT	452BS	322	WALL	35353961	17 MAY 43	CAMBRIDGE
KELLY, PATRICK J. 2/LT	555BS	386	WALL	0-735795	09 AUG 43	CAMBRIDGE
KERN, HERBERT R. S/SGT	535BS	391	WALL	15103843	12 AUG 43	NETHERLANDS
KITTREDGE, DAVID R. S/SGT	450BS	322	WALL	16094800	16 APR 45	NETHERLANDS
LAMBERTSON, HARRY R. S/SGT	558BS	387	WALL	11072004	25 FEB 44	CAMBRIDGE
LAMMERS. ROBERT K. 1/LT	558BS	387	WALL	0-725653	25 FEB 44	NETHERLANDS
LANE, FRANK G. JR. S/SGT	599BS	397	WALL	15354581	23 DEC 44	LUXEMBOURG
LE FAVRE, ARTHUR J. FLT/O	599BS	397	WALL	T-125780	23 DEC 44	LUXEMBOURG
LEACH, DELMAR J. S/SGT	556BS	387	WALL	32078682	09 SEPT 43	ARDENNES
LINDSEY, DARRELL R. CAPT	585BS	394	WALL	0-729031	09 AUG 44	ARDENNES

Name & Rank	Unit	Gp		Number	Date of Death	Cemetery
LINGSLEY, ROBERT E. 1/LT	555BS	386	WALL	0-660573	27 MAY 44	LORRAINE
LITTRELL, MILTON E. S/SGT	450BS	322	WALL	14069802	17 MAY 43	NETHERLANDS
LOOMIS, CLYDE E. JR. 2/LT	450BS	322	WALL	0-682437	08 JUL 44	ARDENNES
MARCHETTI, LEROY P. T/SGT	558BS	387	WALL	31159821	25 FEB 44	NETHERLANDS
MARSZALEK, FRANK S/SGT	553BS	386	WALL	31149602	29 MAY 44	ARDENNES
MATTHEW, FREDERICK H. 1/LT	452BS	322	WALL	0-663062	17 MAY 43	CAMBRIDGE
McCARTER, EDWARD C. S/SGT	495BS	344	WALL	17021312	10 FEB 45	NETHERLANDS
McCASLIN, THOMAS J. S/SGT	555BS	386	WALL	17038437	22 JUN 44	NORMANDY
McCOLLUM, SAMUEL D. 2/LT	553BS	386	WALL	0-731768	30 JUL 43	NETHERLANDS
McGILL, HENRY E. S/SGT	558BS	387	WALL	37370330	25 FEB 44	CAMBRIDGE
McHENRY, JACK 1/LT	558BS	387	WALL	0-742339	15 JUN 44	CAMBRIDGE
McKAMEY, JAMES B. 1/LT	497BS	344	WALL	0-668479	06-JUN 44	NORMANDY
McKINNEY, JAMES F. 2/LT	339BS	319	WALL	0-727035	08 DEC 42	CAMBRIDGE
McMATH, WILLIAM E. S/SGT	453BS	323	WALL	38166658	11 APR 44	CAMBRIDGE
MESEROW, DAVID 1/LT	555BS	386	WALL	0-732880	22 JUN 44	NORMANDY
MICHALOWSKI, CHESTER S/SGT	453BS	323	WALL	36380710	17 FEB 46	LUXEMBOURG
MILLER, HOWARD C. JR. T/SGT	558BS	387	WALL	14128730	25 FEB 44	CAMBRIDGE
MOFFITT, RICHARD C. CAPT	HQ	387	WALL	0-732886	12 APR 44	ARDENNES
MOLNAR, ROBERT S 2/LT	553BS	386	WALL	0-795808	30 JUL 43	NETHERLANDS
MULLINIX, WILLIAM D. 1/LT	558BS	387	WALL	0-742343	25 FEB 44	CAMBRIDGE
NAU, JOHN C. S/SGT	454BS	323	WALL	33173683	11 APR 44	CAMBRIDGE
NEWTON, CHARLES 1/LT	552BS	386	WALL	0-792732	03 JUN 43	CAMBRIDGE
NORTON, EDWARD R. 2/LT	452BS	322	WALL	0-792299	17 MAY 43	NETHERLANDS
O'TOOLE, MARTIN P. 1/LT	454BS	323	WALL	0-671069	11 APR 44	CAMBRIDGE
OGILVIE, WILLIAM S. 2/LT	556BS	387	WALL	0-670595	09 SEPT 43	ARDENNES
OLNEY, HANSFORD G. 1/LT	556BS	387	WALL	0-725032	09 SEPT 43	ARDENNES
PARK, JOHN H. S/SGT	552BS	386	WALL	18130125	08 SEPT 43	CAMBRIDGE
PARKER, RALPH D. JR. S/SGT	587BS	394	WALL	18114908	06 JUN 44	CAMBRIDGE
PARSON, WILLIAM C. 2/LT	440BS	319	WALL	0-727256	08 DEC 42	CAMBRIDGE
PAYNE, BRITTON S/SGT	439BS	319	WALL	36053712	08 DEC 42	CAMBRIDGE
PERKINS, ROBERT E. T/SGT	555BS	386	WALL	33297432	22 JUN 44	NORMANDY
PETERS, FREDERICK E. CAPT	450BS	322	WALL	0-671072	08 JUL 44	ARDENNES
PEW, LEONARD N. CPL	497BS	344	WALL	17129317	28 MAY 44	ARDENNES
PILE, WILLIAM O. 1/LT	559BS	387	WALL	0-686489	23 DEC 44	ARDENNES
PIPHER, GEORGE F. 1/LT	455BS	323	WALL	0-732573	13 DEC 43	NETHERLANDS
POTOMA, MICHAEL S/SGT	440BS	319	WALL	13029793	08 DEC 42	CAMBRIDGE
POWERS, CHARLES D. SGT	553BS	386	WALL	3450789	25 MAR 44	ARDENNES
PRIAR, RICHARD L. S/SGT	453BS	323	WALL	13090857	11 APR 44	CAMBRIDGE
PRUITT, ALBERT L. T/SGT	454BS	323	WALL	38003238	20 MAY 44	ARDENNES
RAYMER, EDWARD H. 2/LT	572BS	391	WALL	0-743686	18 APR 44	ARDENNES
RENEY, ROBERT B. 1/LT	453BS	323	WALL	0-681196	11 APR 44	CAMBRIDGE
REPAR, FRANK J. T/SGT	573BS	391	WALL	20517870	07 AUG 46	ARDENNES
REYNOLDS, CARL E. S/SGT	558BS	387	WALL	33274291	25 FEB 44	CAMBRIDGE
REYNOLDS, JEROME B. 1/LT	450BS	322	WALL	0-727775	09 SEPT 45	ARDENNES
RICE, GEORGE W. S/SGT	558BS	387	WALL	39680110	25 FEB 44	CAMBRIDGE
RICHARDSON, JOSEPH H. MAJ	558BS	387	WALL	0-414402	25 FEB 44	CAMBRIDGE
RICHMOND, MANLEY O. MAJ	573BS	391	WALL	0-401055	17 AUG 45	RHONE
ROBERTSON, GEORGE B. 1/LT	558BS	387	WALL	0-441271	25 FEB 44	CAMBRIDGE
ROGERS, GEORGE S. SGT	587BS	394	WALL	34474119	06 JUN 44	CAMBRIDGE
ROHWEDER, WILLIAM J. S/SGT	597BS	397	WALL	16135719	11 AUG 44	ARDENNES
RYAN, JOHN P. T/SGT	555BS	386	WALL	18061377	09 AUG 43	CAMBRIDGE

Name & Rank	Unit	Gp		Number	Date of Death	Cemetery
SALGADO, JOSEPH F. T/SGT	439BS	319	WALL	06583511	08 DEC 42	CAMBRIDGE
SANCHEZ, JOE R. S/SGT	575BS	391	WALL	39290993	24 DEC 45	LUXEMBOURG
SAYLOR, STERL E. CPL	575BS	391	WALL	12098426	28 APR 45	ARDENNES
SCHARDING, PAUL E. 1/LT	555BS	386	WALL	0-732906	09 AUG 43	CAMBRIDGE
SCHNEIDER, CARROLL R . S/SGT	455BS	323	WALL	19005793	13 DEC 43	NETHERLANDS
SCOTT, JESS R. SGT	497BS	344	WALL	39233319	06 JUN 44	NORMANDY
SHEWELL, JACK C. 2/LT	495BS	344	WALL	0-749337	28 MAY 44	NORMANDY
SHOEMAKER, KENNETH E. 1/LT	573BS	391	WALL	0-699782	07 AUG 46	ARDENNES
SHULER, MELVIN C. SR SGT	573BS	391	WALL	06941952	25 AUG 44	BRITTANY
SIAULINCKAS, STEAVE J. T/SGT	558BS	387	WALL	12078822	25 FEB 44	CAMBRIDGE
SIEVERS, ROBERT L. T/SGT	450BS	322	WALL	36614062	16 APR 45	NETHERLANDS
SLUSTROP, AXEL P. 1/LT	555BS	386	WALL	0-738483	22 JUN 44	NORMANDY
SMITH, EDWARD A. S/SGT	552BS	386	WALL	12049993	03 JUN 43	CAMBRIDGE
SMITH, JOHN L. 1/LT	451BS	322	WALL	0-560349	29 FEB 44	NORMANDY
SMYTH, ARTHUR J. 1/LT	456BS	323	WALL	0-791865	20 MAY 44	ARDENNES
SOUTHWORTH, JESSE W. T/SGT	450BS	322	WALL	33121996	17 MAY 43	NETHERLANDS
ST. PETER, JEROME F. 1/LT	453BS	323	WALL	0-442494	20 MAY 44	CAMBRIDGE
STANDARD, DONALD L. 1/LT	558BS	387	WALL	0-738043	12 APR 44	ARDENNES
STARK, THORNTON W. 1/LT	558BS	387	WALL	0-672242	25 FEB 44	CAMBRIDGE
STEES, MORRIS C. SGT	572BS	391	WALL	33237325	18 APR 44	ARDENNES
STEINBACH, JAMES A. 1/LT	558BS	387	WALL	0-666374	25 FEB 44	CAMBRIDGE
STETSON, LINCOLN H. 1/LT	554BS	386	WALL	0-759318	31 MAR 45	EPINAL
STEVENS, HENRY L. S/SGT	557BS	387	WALL	14042061	23 DEC 44	ARDENNES
STEWART, WILLIAM R. 1/LT	558BS	387	WALL	0-672245	25 FEB 44	CAMBRIDGE
STIRNEMAN, CHARLES H. 1/LT	456BS	323	WALL	0-743864	18 APR 44	ARDENNES
STRAUSS, JOHN A. S/SGT	494BS	344	WALL	12083270	04 JUN 44	CAMBRIDGE
SWALWELL, WARD C. JR. S/SGT	559BS	397	WALL	16137952	23 DEC 44	LUXEMBOURG
TAVENER, CLARK A. 1/LT	575BS	391	WALL	0-757331	23 DEC 44	LUXEMBOURG
THIBAULT, EUGENE F. S/SGT	453BS	323	WALL	11110844	20 MAY 44	CAMBRIDGE
THOMPSON, ALBERT T. JR. S/SGT	556BS	387	WALL	34386282	09 SEPT 43	ARDENNES
TUCKER, DICK A. 1/LT	555BS	386	WALL	0-664696	09 AUG 43	CAMBRIDGE
TURNER, ROBERT W. 2/LT	586BS	394	WALL	0-718806	22 MAR 45	NETHERLANDS
VAN DAMME, WOODROW A. S/SGT	553BS	386	WALL	37180189	25 MAR 44	ARDENNES
VANDER SCHOOT, GERRIT SGT	456BS	323	WALL	36344030	18 APR 44	ARDENNES
VANDLING, JOSEPH T. S/SGT	452BS	322	WALL	13026191	17 MAY 43	CAMBRIDGE
WALLE, WALLACE F. S/SGT	439BS	319	WALL	35300748	08 DEC 42	CAMBRIDGE
WARD, ROBERT W. 2/LT	559BS	387	WALL	0-830759	23 DEC 44	ARDENNES
WATKINS, FRANK L. 2/LT	453BS	323	WALL	20302045	20 MAY 44	ARDENESS
WATSON, JESS A 1/LT	556BS	387	WALL	0-662706	29 NOV 43	NORMANDY
WEISS, DON L. LT/COL	555BS	386	WALL	0-437629	22 JUN 44	NORMANDY
WHEAT, CURTIS E. JR. 1/LT	453BS	323	WALL	0-731349	20 MAY 44	ARDENNES
WILSON, JAMES E. SGT	455BS	323	WALL	38106799	13 DEC 43	NETHERLANDS
WROTEN, ALTON B. 2/LT	574BS	391	WALL	0-718817	24 DEC 45	HENRI & CHAPELLE
YOUNG, JAMES P. S/SGT	553BS	386	WALL	31116149	30 JUL 43	NETHERLANDS
ZIMMERMAN, GLENN F. 1/LT	553BS	386	WALL	0-731721	30 JUL 43	NETHERLANDS
ZUKOSKY, BERNARD T. S/SGT	555BS	386	WALL	13025353	09 AUG 43	CAMBRIDGE

Index

The names in all capital letters are from the cemetery lists or listed on The Walls.

Rousing welcome given to returning Americans

ON one of the biggest days in the history of Silver End, and indeed of all the communities surrounding the second world war airfield of Rivenhall, veterans of the 397th Bomb Group of the 9th USAAF returned.

They visited to commemorate the Friendly Invasion of 50 years ago as American forces arrived in Britain to fight against Hitler.

Forty-five American guests arrived outside the Silver End Hotel and were surprised by the tumultuous reception from the pupils of Silver End Primary School cheering and waving scores of British and American flags.

Pam Bugg, chairman of Silver End Parish Council, greeted them, and Captain George Parker replied for the veterans.

Everybody then walked through the gardens to the Congregational Church, where a fete was in progress.

The sun shone bright on the stalls decorated in red, white and blue, and the children performed maypole and country dancing.

In the church hall Mr Roger DeCoverley held an exhibition of wartime artefacts, many directly related to Rivenhall Airfield.

One veteran was delighted to discover that the photograph that he knew had been taken of his plane, a Martin Marauder, was on display there.

He had been searching American war archives for decades trying to find it. Mr DeCoverley immediately gave the photo to him.

Florida oak trees were planted in the Memorial Gardens and in the grounds of Rivenhall Church to commemorate the visit.

The Florida oak was chosen because it was introduced to this area by the Marauder men when they were stationed here.

Later in the afternoon, the veterans visited the old airfield, where Alan Thorogood, of Marconi Radar Systems, which now occupies the airfield, met them.

Finally, to round off a wonderful day, visitors and locals all gathered in the Silver End Hotel for a buffet and dance.

The music was all 40s songs and melodies. Food was provided by the Friends of Silver End School and the room was decorated in red, white and blue.

June Broad provided some superb flower arrangements.

The evening was designed to gather together the wartime residents of the area to meet the veterans, and the atmosphere was very nostalgic and happy.

Many of the veterans got up and danced to the music, despite all of them being at least 70 years old.

Historian Bruce Stait signed complimentary copies of his history of Rivenhall Airfield for the veterans and an exchange of gifts was made.

The locals presented a photograph of Marauders flying over Coggeshall, and the veterans a print of Marauders over Northern France and a model of the plane.

The evening ended with the national anthems and an emotional rendition of We'll Meet Again as the Americans boarded their coach home.

Jeremy White.

Aérodrome de Lessay

L'émouvant accueil des équipages américains

Quatre mille visiteurs et plus ont foulé l'aérodrome Charles Lindbergh à Lessay hier après-midi. Une grande journée sous le signe du souvenir pour les anciens maraudeurs qui ont fait le débarquement, avec en plus un air de fête autour des équipages de bombardiers et des avions cargos que le public a pu visiter. Le centre aéronautique de Lessay et son président, M.Perdrix, avaient tout mis en oeuvre pour préparer le meilleur accueil aux américains.

Deux aspects donc de cette journée. Tout d'abord des cérémonies officielles pour célébrer le 50ᵉ anniversaire des passages de maraudeurs dans le ciel français. Ces bombardiers américains bimoteurs avaient pour mission à la libération d'appuyer les combats au sol des troupes alliées et leur percée dans les lignes ennemies. Ils bombardaient les points stratégiques allemands.

Certains de ces militaires ont ainsi « visité le ciel de Normandie », a rappelé un officier américain lors des discours, et n'ont foulé le sol français que 50 ans plus tard pour venir commémorer l'histoire de notre libération. Jean-François Legrand, sénateur-maire, a parlé aussi de cette histoire commune entre français et américains écrite page après page depuis Lafayette. « Nous aurons à coeur de continuer à

l'écrire dans la paix. Les enfants des écoles sont venus ici pour témoigner que génération après génération votre combat restera dans nos mémoires ».

Une découverte pour les jeunes, des moments émouvants pour les anciens qui ont vécu en civil ou militaire cette période difficile. Ils étaient tous présents à la levée des drapeaux quand les autorités ont dévoilé la stèle commémorative. Mme Bouvier-Muller, présidente de l'association franco-américaine des aérodromes normands de la 9ᵉ Airforce, a reçu une plaque « en remerciement de ses efforts ».

En fin de cérémonie, le colonel Jacques Choussy est passé avec son avion entre les deux drapeaux encadrant la stèle. M. Choussy est ancien pilote de mirage de l'armée de l'air et aujourd'hui instructeur du club. Les jeunes générations

étaient là aussi pour apporter une note colorée à ce rendez-vous et profiter des animations proposées par le centre : démonstrations d'ULM, de planeurs et des avions du club. Le temps s'y prêtait parfaitement.

Tous n'ont pas manqué de visiter l'avion cargo Transall de la base aérienne d'Evreux qui transportait sa garde d'honneur. Une découverte très impressionnante.

« Nous n'avions pas eu autant de monde depuis le meeting de 1985 et l'anniversaire Charles Lindbergh. Tout le monde a participé à l'organisation de cette journée et particulièrement l'Equipement qui a repeint spécialement les hangars et rénové les abords », a dit le président du centre M.Perdrix.

F.BERRUER

TIMES TO[...]
Facts behind the[...]

A wel[...] old b[...]

by
LARAINE [...]

VILLAGES will be resounding to the beat of the jitterbug and big band music when American veterans return to visit their wartime haunts in May.

Communities across the area are organising themselves into committees to arrange a variety of events to welcome back the lads — and their families — of the Ninth Army Air Force on May 2 and 3.

Villagers in Silver End and Rivenhall have joined forces for their celebrations and have organised themselves into two committees to arrange different events.

An exhibition of memorabilia from the war and, in particular, from the Rivenhall airbase where the 397th Bomb Group was stationed, will be on display in the congregational church hall on May 2.

Most of the collection belongs to local historian Mr Carol De-Coverley who has amassed all sorts of bits and pieces from the airfield, including parts of old planes and the original flag from the base.

There will also be a fete during the afternoon and local organisations such as the Air Training Corps will put up stalls.

One of the organisers, former soldier Phil Shute, said 39 Americans — 23 veterans and their families — were expected, and there could be more.

They will be staying at the Harlequin Hotel at Stansted Airport for the weekend along with the other Marauder Men returning to different parts of Essex for the reunion.

Mr Shute added that he thought many of them

Marau[...]

relive [...]

THEY helped change the course of history and they changed the lives of people in the villages where they stayed.

The Marauder Men marched into "quaint" villages like Earls Colne, with tanned complexions, distinctive accents, money and most of all that brash charm.

Suddenly men like the handsome Hollywood

me for ddies

knew or put up the US servicemen during the war.

In the early evening, the visitors will be taken round any sites they wish to see and then a five-piece band from Kelvedon will strike up the music with some more Glen Miller-style entertainment.

A bar will be manned by the local fire brigade and there will also be a buffet.

Andrewsfield — the first American base to be built in England — will be entertaining 20 former members of the 322 Marauder Bomber squadron and their wives on May 2.

The men of the 381st Bomb Group who were based at Ridgewell will have a taste of medieval Essex when they return as Essex County Council is hoping to organise a tea party for them on Sunday May 3 at Cressing Temple.

The council will be hosting several of the Ma-rauder-Men groups on May 1 at a special reception at County Hall in Chelmsford to which local people will be invited.

• A meeting of the Buddies of the Ninth Association will be held on Sunday at Great Saling village hall at 7pm when Eighth Air Force historian Roger Freeman will give a talk.

USAAF Reunion

RETURN TO ENGLAND 1942-1992

Earl Trull, vétéran de la 9ᵉ Air Force

Earl Trull a troqué son chapeau de cow-boy contre une casquette aux couleurs de la 9ᵉ Air Force. Ce vétéran de 70 ans a quitté quelques jours sa ville natale d'Austin, Texas, pour retrouver le pays où il a fêté son dix-neuvième anniversaire.

En 1944, il faisait partie de l'un des groupes de la 9ᵉ Air Force, basé à Gorges près de Coutances. Avec un fort accent texan, il raconte son aventure « A bord de nos bombardiers moyens B 26 marauders, nous avons quitté notre base anglaise au mois d'août 44 pour rejoindre Gorges, l'une des quatre premières pistes françaises construites dès le début du débarquement avec Maupertus, La-Tour-en-Bessin et Lessay. Les B 26 devaient préparer le terrain devant les armées terrestres ».

A la fin de la guerre, les américains ont jugé que le B 26 était devenu obsolète. « Les avions ont été regroupés sur la base de Francfort. On a mis des explosifs dans les cockpits et on a tout fait sauter ».

Earl Trull revient en France en train et en camion jusqu'au Havre où un bateau l'attend pour le ramener aux Etats-Unis. « Sur le port, beaucoup de pilotes ont laissé des petits chiens qu'ils avaient recueillis. Ils hurlaient sur le quai. Certains ont tout de même caché un chiot dans leur sac pour l'emmener en Amérique », se souvient-il.

De retour aux Etats-Unis, l'adjudant-chef Trull reçoit un beau diplôme avant sa démobilisation : « Depuis ce jour on m'appelle Monsieur », dit-il en riant avant d'ajouter : « Je suis resté dans l'armée quatre ans, sept mois, vingt jours, deux heures et trente minutes ».

Reunion for US war veterans

AMERICAN airmen who were based at Stansted during the war are returning from the United States for a reunion this weekend.

Nearly 2,000 Americans were stationed at Stansted and many of them were with the 344th Bomb Group flying B-26 Martin Marauders on missions across Europe.

Many 344th veterans, some with their wives and families, will be returning on Friday to stay at Stansted's Harlequin Hotel.

Report: DEBBIE BULMER

Some will take part in a plaque unveiling ceremony in the new terminal on Saturday.

The bronze plaque is being presented to Stansted Airport's operations director Ron Paternoster to commemorate the 344th veterans' time at the airport during which time they flew 266 missions into Europe.

Later in the day, the visitors will have a trip to Duxford, followed by a tour of the airport and a chance to identify some of their old locations.

The busy day will also include a tree-planting at the Ash pub, one of the veterans' local haunts back in 1944.

In the evening, the airport sports and social club is hosting a reception for the Americans and invited guests who knew them during their time at Stansted.

er Men emories

ME for heroes awaited world s from the US airforce as they villages and former bases h Essex.

s after they first set foot in the mighty Marauder Men. e B-26 bombers, revisited old ver engraved in their mem-

es of Earls Colne and Ridge-d high on the list of many.

eporter VINCE ELLIS went et the men who all those years

HOTEL REVIVES WAR MEMORIES

HARLEQUIN Hotel staff wore American Air Force uniform when they greeted USAF veteran Marauders who stayed at the hotel last weekend.

The Americans who were based at Stansted during the Second World War have come to be known as the Marauders because they flew B 26 Martin Marauder bomber planes from the Stansted runway.

The veterans came to East Anglia for a week long trip, a reunion to mark the 50th anniversary of their arrival in 1942 at air bases throughout the area.

While at the hotel they admired a model of a Lancaster bomber which was entirely made out of lard and commissioned for the occasion by Head Chef at the hotel, Michael Glynn.

Printed in the USA
CPSIA information can be obtained
at www.ICGtesting.com
JSHW060055150824
68134JS00032B/2741